Samuel

MEN *of* CHARACTER

Samuel

A Lifetime Serving God

GENE A. GETZ

FOREWORD BY BILL BRIGHT

BROADMAN
&HOLMAN
PUBLISHERS

Nashville, Tennessee

© 1997
by Gene A. Getz
Printed in the United States of America

Published by:
Broadman & Holman, Publishers
Nashville, Tennessee
Text Design: Steven Boyd

4261-71
0-8054-6171-1

Dewey Decimal Classification: 248.842
Subject Heading: Samuel, Judge \ Christian Life \ Men—Religious Life
Library of Congress Card Catalog Number: 96–20805

Unless otherwise noted, Scripture quotations are from the Holy Bible, New International Version, copyright © 1973, 1978, 1984 by International Bible Society; other versions used are the New American Standard Bible (NASB), © the Lockman Foundation, 1960, 1962, 1963, 1968, 1971, 1972, 1973, 1975, 1977; used by permission; and the King James Version (KJV).

Library of Congress Cataloging-in-Publication Data
Getz, Gene A.
   [When you're confused & uncertain]
   Samuel: a lifetime serving God / Gene A. Getz.
      p. cm. — (Men of character)
   Originally published : When you're confused & uncertain
   Includes bibliographical references.
   ISBN 0-8054-6167
   1. Bible. O.T. Samuel—Commentaries. I. Title. II. Series: Getz, Gene A.
Men of character.
BS1325.3.G47 1996
222'.406—dc20
96–20805
CIP

1 2 3 4 5 00 99 98 97

I consider it a great privilege to dedicate this book on Samuel's life to a man, who for a number of years has distinguished himself as a great servant of the Lord. I'm speaking of Bill Bright, the founder and director of Campus Crusade for Christ International. Bill's influence and contribution to advancing the kingdom of God was dramatically rewarded when he received the Templeton Prize for progress in religion on May 8, 1996—a prize valued at $1 million, which Bill immediately dedicated to the advancement of prayer.

Bill launched Campus Crusade of Christ International in 1951, and currently the influence of this ministry literally reaches around the world through more than forty separate ministries. Millions have come to know the Lord Jesus Christ personally through a simple approach to presenting the gospel—an approach developed by Bill more than forty years ago. I'm speaking of his *Four Spiritual Laws* booklet which states:

Law 1: God loves you and offers a wonderful plan for your life (John 3:16; 10:10).

Law 2: Man is sinful and separate from God. Thus he cannot know and experience God's love and plan for his life (Rom. 3:23; 6:23).

Law 3: Jesus Christ is God's only provision for man's sin. Through Him you can know and experience God's love and plan for your life (Rom. 5:8; 1 Cor. 15:3–6).

Law 4: We must individually receive Jesus Christ as Savior and Lord. Then we can know and experience God's love and plan for our lives (John 1:12; Eph. 2:8–9; John 3:1–8; Rev. 3:20).

Thanks, Bill, for your vision, and for your commitment, which has translated your vision into reality. In my eyes—and in the eyes of millions of other men and women—you're a man of character. You've demonstrated with your life that it's possible to "fix our eyes on Jesus, the author and perfecter of our faith" (Heb. 12:2). God bless you, my friend. It is indeed a privilege to dedicate this book to you.

Gene Getz

Contents

Foreword

I am grateful that my dear friend, Gene Getz, has dedicated this volume to me, and I am privileged that he has asked me to write the foreword.

His dedicatory words are humbling. I thank our wonderful Lord and Savior Jesus Christ for anything I have been able to accomplish. I give Him all the glory for the worldwide ministry of Campus Crusade for Christ.

Gene's words and this book are also challenging. They make me want all the more to be faithful to the Lord's calling, without deviation, and to be a man of faith and character, as are the biblical examples of whom Gene writes.

I cannot say that I have served the Lord since childhood, like Samuel, because I did not come to Christ until after college. Since that time, some fifty years ago, however, I have pledged to serve my Lord joyfully as long as He gives me breath.

After attending college in my home state of Oklahoma, I moved to California and started what became a successful business. I was driven by personal ambition, and I was the center of my own universe. But through the influence of the Hollywood Presbyterian Church and my mother's prayers, I discovered the great Creator God of the universe and what He had done for me through His only begotten Son. My life wonderfully changed, and I purposed in my heart to serve Him forever.

Both my beloved wife, Vonette, and I had been very materialistic in our youth. When we received Christ as our Lord and Savior, however, we began to discover many things that were far more important than making money, living in lovely homes, and enjoying "the good life," which I had promised her when I proposed to her.

But within a couple of years, our desires and interests had changed. Vonette was a vital part of everything I was doing, and together we came to the conclusion that knowing and serving Jesus was more important than anything in the world. So on a Sunday afternoon in the spring of 1951, in our home in the Hollywood Hills, Vonette and I got on our knees and prayed, "Lord, we surrender our lives to Your will. We will go where You want us to go and do what You want us to do. We want to be Yours completely, irrevocably."

God has blessed us and the ministry He gave us forty-five years ago, Campus Crusade for Christ, above measure. By God's grace, and with help from our wonderful board of directors and supporters throughout the world, Vonette and I and our staff have since had the privilege of working together with millions of Christians in thousands of churches of all denominations and hundreds of missions groups, whom we have helped to train. In helping to fulfill the Great Commission, Campus Crusade for Christ now has more than forty separate ministries dedicated to that one objective; nearly thirteen thousand full-time staff members and approximately 101,000 trained associates and volunteer staff members in one hundred sixty-five countries. We have had the privilege of helping take the gospel to well over two billion people, and tens of millions have indicated salvation decisions. Again, I'm thankful Gene Getz has dedictated this volume to me, and I want to give our Lord all the glory. In turn, I am thankful for Gene and his writing skills, as well as his commitment to pastoring and leading a large body of believers at Fellowship Bible Church North, which is just one of many Fellowship churches he has pastored and helped start. The *Men of Character* series is a great contribution to edifying the body of

Christ, particularly at this time when the Holy Spirit is moving so dramatically among men around the world. This book on Samuel contributes greatly to this whole series.

Dr. Bill Bright
Founder and President
Campus Crusade for Christ International

Introduction

A Lifetime Serving God

*S*eldom do we meet men who have served God for a lifetime—even those who have become our biblical heroes. Samuel beats the odds! He "continued to grow . . . in favor with the LORD *and with men*" (1 Sam. 2:26) from the time he was a small child until he went home to be with God at a ripe old age. He bypassed adolescent rebellion and never went through a midlife crisis! He served God and Israel all of his life.

This does not mean that Samuel never faced a crisis in his ministry. As a young adolescent, he may have erred in sending the army of Israel to do battle with the Philistines. Most of the crises he faced, however, were not of his own doing.

Samuel probably experienced his greatest emotional pain when God's rebellious people replaced this faithful servant with a king. Though God assured this old prophet and dynamic leader that Israel had rejected Him instead of Samuel, he still felt the sting that accompanies this kind of rejection.

In spite of this difficult period in his life, Samuel remained faithful to Israel. Though he was set aside as their primary leader, he never ceased praying for his people and never stopped teaching them God's will when the opportunity came his way.

A Great Need Today

Today we need men of character—men like Samuel, who are born into Christian homes, who have accepted Christ early in their lives, and who have served the Lord all the days of their lives. However, many of us didn't even know about Jesus Christ until we were up in years. Others of us knew about the Lord and even accepted Him as personal Savior, but we walked out of His will for a period of time before we—like the prodigal son—returned to our Father.

However, no matter what our background, we can join men like the apostle Paul, who as an adult acknowledged his terrible sin against Jesus Christ and His church (1 Tim. 1:12–17), and stated for all to read and to hear: "Forgetting what is behind and straining toward what is ahead, I press on toward the goal to win the prize for which God has called me heavenward in Christ Jesus" (Phil. 3:13–14).

This is the wonderful message of the Word of God. No matter what our past, we can begin at any moment in our lives and become men of character.

Chapter 1

Chaos and Confusion
Read Judges 21:25

Once when my wife and I were in England, we visited the great Salisbury Cathedral—a gigantic structure that boasts the highest tower and steeple in Europe. The tower and spire rise more than four hundred feet above the ground and are visible for miles. The tower and spire alone weigh more than 6,400 tons. Begun early in the thirteenth century, the cathedral still stands as a testimony to the architectural skills of people who knew nothing of our modern ways and means of building.

Amazingly, this enormous structure is built on only a four-foot foundation. Underneath this shallow base lies a deep bed of gravel saturated with water that emanates from several rivers. Should the water ever drain from this gravel bed, the whole substructure of this four-foot foundation will deteriorate and crumble. The whole building will come crashing down. That's why the water level is monitored regularly, even though it has probably never varied for millennia.

As I reflected on this incredible phenomenon, I thought about our nation. We stood firm for many years until the "water of life"—our biblical values as embodied in the Ten Commandments—were drained from this simple yet profound substructure upon which we built our nation. Amazingly, this change took place in only one generation.

How could this have happened? The fact is that this kind of degeneration is nothing new in history. It happened again and again to the children of Israel, and when it did, the whole culture deteriorated and chaos permeated the lives of God's people.

A Low Point

Samuel was born at a time in Israel's history when confusion reigned. The concluding line in the book of Judges says it all: "Everyone did as he saw fit." (Judg. 21:25). The New American Standard translation describes the scene more graphically: "Everyone did what was right in his own eyes."

What made this situation so chaotic is not only that the children of Israel "had no king" but that they had consistently slid back into a state of paganism. The Book of Judges is basically a record of Israel's "ups and downs"—turning from their sins to worship the one true God and then turning from God to worship the false gods of Canaan.

A Powerful Sermon

Just before he died, Joshua had warned God's people and had challenged them to "fear the LORD" and to "serve Him with all faithfulness!" (Josh. 24:14). More specifically, this great man exhorted them with these words: "Throw away the gods your forefathers worshiped beyond the River and in Egypt, and serve the LORD. But if serving the LORD seems undesirable to you, then choose for yourselves this day whom you will serve, whether the gods your forefathers served beyond the River, or the gods of the Amorites, in whose land you are living" (24:14–15a).

Joshua concluded this very pointed message with a personal testimony regarding his own decision—a powerful witness that any godly father would be proud to have inscribed as an epitaph on his own tombstone: "But as for me and my household, we will serve the Lord" (24:15b).

Good News, Bad News

Though the children of Israel responded very positively to Joshua's exhortation and personal example (24:16–24), they failed to follow through. The *good news* is that they "served the Lord throughout the lifetime of Joshua and of the elders who outlived him and who had seen all the great things the Lord had done for Israel" (Judg. 2:7). The *bad news* is that after Joshua died and "after that whole generation had been gathered to their fathers, another generation grew up, who knew neither the LORD nor what He had done for Israel" (2:10). Following are the saddest words ever penned regarding Israel's history: "Then the Israelites did evil in the eyes of the LORD and served the Baals. They forsook the LORD, the God of their fathers, who had brought them out of Egypt. They followed and worshiped various gods of the peoples around them. They provoked the LORD to anger because they forsook him and served Baal and the Ashtoreths" (2:11–13).

In only one generation, a whole new group of Israelites replaced their fathers and mothers and turned to paganism. They actually forgot what God had done in delivering their forefathers from Egyptian bondage, as well as miraculously leading their parents across Jordan and enabling them to conquer the land of Canaan.

How can we explain this? The answer is really simple—although startling and convicting (see fig. 1.1). After Joshua's death, his own generation served God as they said they would. But not so their children. This generation of young people allowed the pagan influences in Canaan to penetrate their thinking and the way they lived. It certainly happened gradually and subtly—like the proverbial frog in a kettle of water that gradually reaches a boiling point. Furthermore, when this new generation produced offspring (the next generation), they failed to review for their children what God had done for them, nor did they instruct this generation in God's holy laws and commandments. In only one generation the children of Israel moved from serving God and obeying His commandments to following false gods and living sinful and licentious lives.

The Process of Degeneration in Israel

Joshua's Generation
The people served the Lord (Judg. 2:7).

The Next Generation
They failed to model and teach their children (2:10).

The Next Generation
They did evil in the sight of the Lord and served the Baals (2:11).

Figure 1.1

In Retrospect

Let's go back to the generation that lived after Joshua's generation. The children of Israel had wandered in the wilderness for forty years because of their unwillingness to take possession of the land of Canaan. Moses then gathered the new generation of Israelites together and reviewed for them what had happened to their parents and why they had died over this forty-year period without entering the Promised Land. They had failed to trust and obey God. But Joshua and Caleb were exceptions. They survived God's purging process in the wilderness because they alone out of twelve spies had wanted to obey God (Num. 14:38).

Moses' Review

Israel's faithful leader also reviewed God's laws. This is the purpose of Deuteronomy, the fourth book in the Old Testament. The term itself is derived from two Greek words, *deuteros*, meaning "second," and *nomos*, meaning "law." Hence, the title "Deuteronomy" literally means "second law." In actuality, this book is a record of Moses' sermons on the moral and civil laws which Israel received at Mt. Sinai.

"Be Careful to Obey"

There is no more powerful and important chapter in the Old Testament than chapter six in the book of Deuteronomy. It's the key to understanding Israel's tragic history described in the book of Judges. From a positive point of view, this chapter contains the secret to living a long and fruitful life—as individuals, as families, and as a larger corporate community. With concise clarity, Moses reminded all who could understand that what he was about to say regarding God's "commands," "decrees," and "laws" were written that Israel's "children and their children after them [the next generation] may fear the Lord" (6:2). He did not want this new generation of Israelites to repeat their parents' mistakes. Consequently, he asked for their undivided attention. "Hear O Israel," Moses proclaimed, "and be careful to obey so that it may go well with you" (6:3).

"Love the Lord Your God"

Moses reminded Israel that their obedience was to be based on their love for God—not just some simple verbal assent, but love that flowed from their total being and which recognized that the Lord who brought them out of Egypt was the only true God. Thus, he again proclaimed, "Hear, O Israel: The LORD our God, the LORD is one. Love the LORD your God with all your heart and with all your soul and with all your strength. These commandments that I give you today are to be upon your hearts" (Deut. 6:4–6).

"Impress Them on Your Children"

At this juncture, Moses clearly outlined his major concern. He knew that once this new generation of Israelites settled in the land, they would be tempted to forget to pass God's commandments on to their children. Consequently, he became very specific: "These commandments that I give you today are to be upon your hearts. Impress them on your children. Talk about them when you sit at home and when you walk along the road, when you lie down and when you get up. Tie them as symbols on your hands and bind them on your foreheads. Write them on the doorframes of your houses and on your gates" (6:6–9).

There is no way anyone can improve on this approach to biblical education. These parents were to take advantage of the natural opportunities in the context of life. They were to use every moment of every day to communicate their own love for God and their commitment to keeping His commandments. All other education was to build on this dynamic foundation laid down by God-fearing parents.

Don't misunderstand. This does not mean they sat with pointed fingers exhorting their children from morning to night. Rather, they were to consistently demonstrate their own love for God throughout the day. They were to model godliness in their marital and family relationships and with their neighbors. And when natural opportunities arose—and they did everyday—they were to share God's Word with deep conviction.

One Moonlit Night

I remember one experience I had with my own children that I almost missed. For several summers, my wife and I had the opportunity to serve on the counseling staff at Word of Life Island in upstate New York. On one occasion, we had arrived early to get settled. That first evening we walked together to the beach area.

It was a beautiful moonlit night with stars so bright it seemed you could reach out and touch them. Suddenly, I realized this was an opportunity that rarely came my way—an opportunity to worship God together as a family in that great outdoor cathedral! I hurriedly started a fire, while my wife, Elaine, went back to the cabin to get some marshmallows. As we sat together that beautiful evening, we sang some worship songs and talked about God's great creation.

I'll never forget my oldest daughter's prayer that evening. In her own eight-year-old way, she stood facing the lake. Over the water you could see the shimmering reflections of the lights from the town of Schroon Lake, nearly a mile away. Looking up into the starry sky, she thanked God for His great power in creating all of this beauty. Then she thanked God most of all that we could be together as a family.

That moment is indelibly etched in my memory. To think, as a father I almost missed the opportunity to do what Moses had commanded the children of Israel to do so many years ago. There was no way I could ever recreate that kind of teaching and worship experience!

"Be Careful That You Do Not Forget the Lord"

Moses knew what lay ahead for Israel. They were going to inherit a land that had "large, flourishing cities" that they did not have to construct. They would receive "houses filled with all kinds of good things." They would drink from wells they "did not dig" and harvest grapes and olives from "vineyards and olive groves" they didn't even plant (6:10–11).

Moses also knew that if this happened, they would be tempted to "forget the LORD" who had delivered them from Egyptian bondage (6:12). They would not only fail to remember what God had done for them; but they would be tempted to take the next step and follow after the false gods of Canaan—to bow down to idols of wood and stone.

Later in this powerful and penetrating message to Israel, Moses reiterated his concerns but added one other fatal ingredient in this process of forgetting what God had done for them. "Your heart will become proud," Moses warned, and they would even take credit for what they had so freely received

(8:14–16). "You may say to yourself, 'my power and the strength of my hands have produced this wealth for me'" (8:17).

In this study of Samuel's life and ministry, we'll see this sin tragically illustrated in the life of Saul once he was anointed king of Israel. It was pride and arrogance that turned his world upside down, and that led to his downfall and terrible death on the battlefield. He ended up committing suicide.

Practice First, Preach Second

The children of Israel remembered these exhortations and obeyed them all during Joshua's tenure as Moses' successor. This happened primarily because Joshua was a faithful leader in Israel. He listened well to Moses' warnings and instructions. First, he personally obeyed the law of God. He did not "turn from it to the right or to the left" (Josh. 1:7). He was a godly model.

But there was a second reason Israel followed the Lord. Joshua faithfully reviewed God's will for the children of Israel. He did not allow the "book of the law" to depart from his mouth. He meditated "on it day and night" so that he could not only obey God's Word in his own life, but also communicate these great truths to Israel (1:8). Joshua first *practiced*, and then he *preached!*

"They Forsook the LORD"

Unfortunately, the generation that emerged following Joshua's death did exactly what both Moses and Joshua had warned against! They failed to love the LORD their God with all their hearts. Predictably, when this happened, they did not review for their children what God had done for them, nor did they teach them God's Laws. Consequently, they "did evil in the eyes of the LORD and served the Baals. They forsook the LORD, the God of their fathers, who had brought them out of

Egypt" (Judg. 2:11). The Book of Judges records this tragic three-hundred-year history in Israel.

God's Grace Through Samuel

Though God became very angry with the children of Israel, He never turned His back on their cry for help. When they were captured by their pagan neighbors and fell into bondage, God again and again raised up judges to deliver them when they "cried out" to Him! Unfortunately, they repeated the same pattern and "did evil in the eyes of the LORD" many times (3:12). And even though they turned back to God, with each flip-flop, the children of Israel spiraled downward (see fig. 1.2).

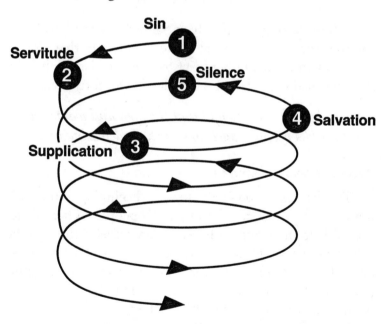

Figure 1.2
**Israel's History as Depicted
in the Book of Judges**

When the nation reached its lowest point, God once again revealed His compassion and grace. Samuel, who was destined to be a man of character, was born and served as a godly influence among the children of Israel for years to come.

Regarding this unique event, Eugene Merrill states: "Just when it seemed the nation would cave in on its own rottenness, God intervened and in response to godly Hannah's prayer gave young Samuel to her and the nation. Samuel's strong leadership as judge, prophet and priest provided respite to the people for both their internal and external threat."[1]

Becoming God's Man Today

Principles to Live By

Before looking specifically at Samuel's miraculous birth, consider some very practical biblical principles that already stand out from this rather brief overview of Israel's history after they had wandered in the wilderness for forty years.

Principle 1. It is God's will that the men and women who lead His people model consistent, God-fearing lives.

Needed: Men of Character

This has been God's plan from the beginning of time. He wants "men of character" to lead His people. When Moses needed help in governing Israel as they traveled through the wilderness, he was to "select *capable men* from all the people— men who *fear God, trustworthy* men who hate dishonest gain" (Exod. 18:21, emphasis mine). They were to be "wise, understanding and respected men" (Deut. 1:13).

When Paul instructed Timothy to appoint elders and deacons in the church, he was to look for men who had good reputations among both Christians and non-Christians and men who were morally pure. They were to be men who were "temperate, self-controlled, respectable, hospitable, able to teach, not given to drunkenness, not violent but gentle, not quarrelsome, not a lover of money" (1 Tim. 3:1–3).

Satan's Strategy Today

Without godly leaders, God's people go astray. They have no models of righteousness. They have no one to teach them how to live consistent Christian lives. This is why Satan has made a concerted attack on pastors and Christian leaders today. When leaders fail, the body of Christ is seriously threatened. Furthermore, those who are non-Christians often become more cynical and convinced that Christianity is just another religion and the church of Jesus Christ is filled with hypocrites.

I'll never forget the day I sat in the Kansas City airport watching a newscast on television. Another TV evangelist had just fallen morally. People all around me were reflecting various reactions—snickers, disgust, and shock. Sadly, some simply responded with a "ho-hum" attitude, as if to say, "Why be surprised? All religious leaders are hypocrites!"

A Reassuring Experience!

I was saddened that day but also challenged and encouraged in my own life. In a few minutes, I got on a plane and flew to Colorado to join some friends on the ski slopes. The next day I met a stranger on one run down the mountain. As we stopped to admire the view, it was not surprising that this man turned the conversation to the immoral behavior of this TV evangelist, but then he said something that encouraged me greatly. Though he had not yet become a Christian, he mentioned he had been watching Billy Graham on television for several years. "There's a man," he said, "who represents what Christianity is all about!"

At that moment in my life when I felt all non-Christians were looking askance at those of us in the ministry, I realized how one consistent Christian leader can impact others—even overcoming the devastating impact of hypocrisy.

Modeling consistency is an awesome principle, and very convicting for any serious-minded teacher of the Word of God. I know it is in my own life since no one knows how human I really am except me! James adds to the power and penetrating conviction of this principle when he wrote, "Not many of you should presume to be teachers, my brothers, because you know that we who teach will be judged more strictly" (James 3:1).

Principle 2. Having God-fearing leaders who model and teach the truth does not guarantee that God's people will always live in God's will.

All of us have a free will. We can choose to obey or disobey. Joshua made this point clear when he charged the children of Israel in one of his final sermons: "Choose for yourselves this day whom you will serve" (Josh. 24:15). Joshua also made it clear he had already made his choice when he proclaimed, "But as for me and my household, we will serve the LORD."

Bad Choices

In spite of both Moses' and Joshua's godly leadership, the children of Israel still chose to disobey and to suffer the consequences in their lives and in the lives of their children. Unfortunately, this is true even in our Christian families today. Children grow up and make choices that lead them out of the will of God.

As pastors and parents, we must understand and accept this principle. No matter how faithful we are, some people—even our own children—may not respond. But if we have failed to be the model we should be, we must never rationalize away our weaknesses. We must admit our mistakes and do what we can to correct them. When we have done the best we can, we must leave the results to God. As a loving heavenly Father, He will eventually discipline His wayward children. When He does, He will get their attention, even though we cannot.

Principle 3. Men who are chosen to lead God's people— even by God Himself—do not always remain faithful and free from sin and failure.

The Scriptures are replete with illustrations of failure among leaders. Even Moses made a serious mistake in the homestretch of his life, and though God loved him dearly, He did not allow him to enter the Promised Land.

Early in our study of Samuel's life, we will meet Eli, a "great high priest" in Israel and Samuel's mentor, but a man who failed to restrain his own sons and suffered some very painful results. What can we say as well about Samson, King Saul, King David, and his son Solomon? They all failed God miserably.

These examples provide great lessons for all of us. To quote Paul: "If you think you are standing firm, be careful that you don't fall!" (1 Cor. 10:12). Paul also instructed us that this is why God has recorded these events in such graphic detail (1 Cor. 10:6–11). But let's remember that Paul also concluded this paragraph in the Corinthian letter with some great news: "No temptation has seized you except what is common to man. And God is faithful; He will not let you be tempted beyond what you can bear. But when you are tempted, He will also provide a way out so that you can stand up under it" (1 Cor. 10:13).

We *can* be overcomers. God has provided us with the resources we need to defeat Satan. We can put on God's armor and withstand the devil's evil darts (Eph. 6:10–18).

Principle 4. It is clear from history that it only takes one generation for degeneration to take place among God's people.

This principle is graphically illustrated in Israel's history following Joshua's death. Ironically, this is exactly what has happened in our own culture. There is no question that

America was founded by godly men, many of whom were born-again Christians. And even those who did not claim to know the Lord Jesus Christ as personal Savior believed and taught the values outlined in both the Old and New Testaments. Even Thomas Jefferson, an outspoken deist, upheld the Hebrew-Christian ethic.

For years Americans utilized this standard in their personal, business, and religious lives. But in the 1960s a decided change took place. The Supreme Court no longer considered the values of our founding fathers a major criteria for making judicial decisions. The majority of those who served us in the highest legal body of our nation believed we had progressed beyond this outdated approach to life.

Since that time we have seen an unbelievable deterioration take place in our culture. Drug abuse has become rampant. Adultery and premarital sex have become accepted norms. Families are blowing apart. Abortion is a common practice. Homosexuality has become an accepted lifestyle. Pornography is available on every street corner, in sophisticated hotels, and on the Internet. Rape, child abuse, wife abuse, and murder are on the increase! These realities are not just the babblings of pastors and theologians. They are a matter of public record. It is even illegal in some sectors to display the Ten Commandments on the walls in our public schools.

How long, may I ask, has this process taken? The answer is obvious. It has been one generation. What happened to Israel is happening in our own society. Furthermore, it will happen to any nation where biblical values are not modeled and taught.

Principle 5. In spite of horrible failure and sin, God is merciful and responds when His people confess their sins and cry out for help.

This is the good news that permeates the book of Judges. In spite of Israel's persistent failure, God responded when they cried for help.

We Can Make a Difference

Today, God will respond to us if we pray for our nation. He may not ultimately deliver America from deterioration, disintegration, and destruction if our leaders continue to "stiff arm" the Lord, the God who made our nation strong. But those of us who have "never bowed the knee to Baal" can be assured that God has not forgotten us. He who "lives within us is greater than he who lives in the world." We have His Word. We are part of the body of Jesus Christ, His church. We have an environment where we can grow and model and teach God's truth to our children—within our family structures as well as within the church. If we follow His principles, we can be victorious over sin and Satan. This is what this "men of character" series is all about.

Personalizing These Principles

Following are some questions to help you apply these principles to your own life:

1. As a pastor or parent, am I modeling consistent Christian living before those who look to me for guidance?

2. If I am not succeeding in leading "my sheep" or "my children" in the ways of God, have I evaluated why—realizing that God does not guarantee 100 percent response to my efforts? At the same time, am I rationalizing my failure?

3. As a pastor or parent, am I on guard against Satan who has one major goal—to cause me to fail God by yielding to sin's temptation and in so doing, disillusion those who have been looking to me for spiritual guidance?

4. As I look at my own family of believers or at my own children, am I aware of the influence of worldly values

on their lives? Am I doing all I can in a *proactive* rather than a *reactive* way to counter these negative influences?

5. Am I doing all I can to support a ministry to children, both in my own family and within the church?

Set a Goal

As you reflect on these principles, ask the Holy Spirit to reveal to you what one goal you need to set for your life?

_____

_____

_____

_____

Memorize the Following Scripture

For no one can lay any foundation other than the one already laid, which is Jesus Christ. If any man builds on this foundation using gold, silver, costly stones, wood, hay or straw, his work will be shown for what it is, because the Day will bring it to light. It will be revealed with fire, and the fire will test the quality of each man's work.

1 Corinthians 3:11–13

Growing Together

The following questions are designed for small group discussion:

1. What unique opportunities has God given you to model and teach Christian truths to others—either to your children or to your brothers and sisters in Christ?

2. What opportunities have you missed? Can you think of some ways to recapture these opportunities?

3. In what ways are you supporting your pastor in order to help protect him from Satan's evil attacks? How can we as men support our pastors so they are not overcome with various kinds of temptations?

4. What can we do as men to help reverse the negative trend in our society without violating our priorities in our families and in our church?

5. In what way can we pray for you personally?

Chapter 2

A Cry for Help
Read 1 Samuel 1:1–20

*T*he week I was reflecting on Samuel's birth and the intense emotions surrounding this event, I could not help but notice the following letter written to Ann Landers:

> Last week, I gave birth to my fourth daughter. My husband and I are thrilled to have four healthy girls, but my father-in-law is disappointed. He has offered me $10,000 to "try again" and produce a boy.
> I am outraged. My husband says I'm overreacting. Am I?
> Baltimore "Betty"
> Dear Betty:
> Outrage takes energy. Ignore the clod. Sounds like strudel in the noodle to me.[1]

History Repeats Itself

In addition to this father-in-law's embarrassing immaturity in this letter and the humor in Ann's response, I was intrigued by some of the correlations between family dynamics in the twentieth century and the family dynamics that have existed since the dawn of creation. There is no group of human beings that harbors more anxiety, frustration, anger, and other forms of emotional pain than the family unit. On the positive side, there are no relationships that can bring more joy, happiness, peace, and other positive emotions than this God-ordained institution. And as most of us know, these positive and negative emotions are often mingled together and are sometimes difficult to untangle. Ironically, even "love" and "hate" seem to run on the same relational track.

Family dysfunction is not a new phenomena. It permeates the history of the Old Testament, demonstrating the reality of sin in the world. The Scriptures are honest and open about these realities. There are no "cover-ups." Bible authors do not make God's people look good by hiding the facts. As we'll see in this study, Samuel's family is no exception. The story of his birth unfolds in the midst of a turbulent family unit, and as we look at this story, we'll understand why.

A Two-Woman Man

Samuel's father was Elkanah and his mother was Hannah (1 Sam. 1:1–2). But the biblical text is clear that all was not well in this Jewish household before Samuel was born. Elkanah had two wives; and to complicate matters, Peninnah "had children, but Hannah had none" (1:2).

God often tolerated polygamy in the Old Testament, but it was not His perfect will. Wherever it existed, the normal problems in any monogamous marriage are not only doubled but multiplied many times.

A Religious Man

In spite of Elkanah's failures, he was still a deeply religious man (1:3). He had not forsaken the one true God to worship the "gods" of Canaan like so many of his fellow Israelites. Evidently, he faithfully celebrated all three special feasts outlined by the Lord in the book of Exodus (23:15–16).

"Three times a year," God had said, "all the men are to appear before the Sovereign Lord" (23:17). Though many in

Israel failed to honor God in this way—just as many Christians today fail to honor God by worshiping Him regularly and giving the first fruits of their material possessions—Elkanah was very conscientious about obeying these particular commandments. We read that "year after year this man went up from his town to worship and sacrifice to the LORD Almighty at Shiloh" (1 Sam. 1:3).

Favoritism and Retaliation

Twice in this text we're told that "the LORD had closed" Hannah's womb (1:5–6). Does this mean that Hannah was cursed by God and that her barrenness resulted from some specific sin in her own life? I don't think so. Like the man born blind that John described in his gospel (John 9:1–3), it simply indicates that God is sovereign, even in our physical problems. Though God had warned the children of Israel He would cause barrenness among them if they disobeyed Him (Deut. 28:4, 18), we have no strong evidence in this story that Hannah was the victim of this curse. She was probably unable to bear children just as many women—even Christian women today—have difficulty conceiving.

On the other hand, Hannah no doubt felt despised and rejected by God, especially since her rival kept taunting her and reminding her of her condition. Perhaps Peninnah even paraded her own ability to have children as a blessing from God. Elkanah, however, did not view her in this way. He dearly loved Hannah. He demonstrated this love by giving her a "double portion" of the meat.

Predictably, this angered Peninnah. Though she had provoked and irritated Hannah all along because of her barrenness, Peninnah "doubled" her efforts when Elkanah "doubled" Hannah's portions. In fact, Peninnah's verbal abuse was so intense and painful for Hannah that she often burst into tears and became so emotionally distraught she couldn't even eat—

a sign of intense anxiety and depression. To make matters worse, this "went on year after year" (1 Sam. 1:7).

A Typical Male Response

I find Elkanah's response to Hannah's emotional pain both humorous and embarrassing, simply because most of us—including "yours truly"—have tried to comfort our wives in the same way. His four questions reflect his inability to relate to her feelings:

- *Hannah, why are you weeping?* [As if he didn't know.]
- *Why don't you eat?* [As if he didn't understand the reason.]
- *Why are you downhearted?* [Again, as if he wasn't aware of what was happening.]
- *Don't I mean more to you than ten sons* (1:8)?

Elkanah's final question lets us peer into his own heart. He was threatened. He definitely felt that his efforts at loving Hannah were being rejected and ignored. In some respects, they were, but at this moment Hannah wanted empathy and sincere understanding. She didn't want Elkanah's self-centered approach to her problem, which characterized his questions. Though sincere, he was trying to tell Hannah that she had no reason to feel so sad since she had him. Sound familiar?

Elkanah had just added to Hannah's emotional turmoil. She was probably on a guilt trip already for not being able to handle her negative emotions, and he had just intensified her problem. It's obvious from what happened next that his approach didn't ease her pain whatsoever.

A Painful Cry for Help

One of the great benefits that accompanies this kind of emotional pain is that it "drives us to our knees." This is what happened to Hannah. On one occasion, while worshiping in Shiloh, she opened her heart before God and cried out to Him for help:

"In bitterness of soul Hannah wept much and prayed to the LORD. And she made a vow, saying, "O LORD Almighty, if you will only look upon your servant's misery and remember me, and not forget your servant but give her a son, then I will give him to the LORD for all the days of his life, and no razor will ever be used on his head" (1:10–11).

A Broken Heart

To cry out to God for a son "in bitterness of soul" indicates the depth of Hannah's emotional pain and misery. Furthermore, to offer to give a son to the Lord "all the days of his life" demonstrates an unselfish heart and unusually pure motives, but also her desperation! She personally wanted the joy of bringing a child into the world, which is understandable; but on the other hand, she was willing to give him back to God.

Though we often use this passage when parents dedicate their children to the Lord in a special service of consecration, Hannah had more in mind than simply "giving" a son to the Lord as an act of commitment. She was referring to the Nazirite vow described in the Book of Numbers—a commitment that demanded a number of stringent requirements (Num. 6:1–8).

A Broken Vow

Remember Samson? He was God's "Superman"—until he violated the Nazirite vow. He lost his incredible strength when the Philistines shaved his head (Judg. 16:1–22). Under almost identical circumstances, his parents made the same vow to God as Hannah (13:2–5). Samson's mother also was barren. Samson, too, was a miracle child.

Normally, the Nazirite vow was voluntary (Num. 6:1). It could be taken for a specific period of time with the freedom to terminate this commitment. But in Hannah's case, if God gave her a son, she was willing to make a vow that would be binding "all the days" of this boy's life (1 Sam. 1:12). Again this indicates her degree of commitment to God in exchange for the blessing of bearing a son.

A Pathetic Picture

Hannah's prayer was so intense and persistent that Eli, the high priest in Israel, thought she was drunk. In actuality, she was "praying in her heart, and her lips were moving but her voice was not heard" (1 Sam. 1:13).

Think for a moment what had just happened. Hannah's husband had not handled her emotions well. And now her "pastor" exhorted her to clean up her act and stop drinking! With no understanding whatsoever, Eli—the high priest in Israel—told her, "Get rid of your wine" (1:14).

It's difficult to describe the pain Hannah must have felt. She was down on herself already. She probably believed God had cursed her. Her rival had provoked her to tears, her husband had misunderstood her, and now Eli had condemned her. What a pathetic picture!

But Hannah defended herself nobly, though emotionally. When falsely accused, she quickly set the record straight and informed Eli that she was not intoxicated. "Do not take your servant for a wicked woman," she sobbed. "I have been praying here out of my great anguish and grief" (1:16).

A Miracle Child

Though Eli was initially blunt and insensitive, underneath he was a compassionate and insightful man. He quickly recognized his blunder. When he saw beyond Hannah's outward appearance and into her heart, he was deeply moved. He sensed her sincerity and he joined her in prayer, asking God to grant her request (1:17).

Eli's sympathetic response and spiritual concern lifted Hannah's spirits. Miraculously, her depression subsided, her anguish dissipated—and she even sat down and enjoyed a meal (1:18).

Interestingly, she seems to have known that God had heard these prayers. When she returned home, she conceived and gave birth to a son she named Samuel—a name that would constantly remind everyone who met him that he was another miracle child in Israel—a definite answer to specific prayer (1:20).

Becoming God's Man Today

Principles to Live By

Though the events in this Old Testament story may seem far removed from our twentieth-century way of life, yet we can learn timeless principles that are just as relevant today as they were centuries ago.

Principle 1. It's easy to carry out the external requirements of Christianity yet neglect the internal and foundational requirements which give meaning to our outward forms of worship and commitment.

Elkanah was a religious man—a faithful Jew when it came to performing the outward requirements of the law, particularly in terms of offering sacrifices to God. However, when it came to matters of the heart, he allowed the world's system to penetrate his lifestyle. We must remember that in this moment of Israel's history, "everyone did as he saw fit" (Judg. 21:25), including marrying more than one woman. Elkanah's decision to be a polygamist and to subsequently demonstrate favoritism toward Hannah definitely reflected the pagan influence that had penetrated his own life. Consequently, he suffered the consequences in terms of his family life.

Externalism Without Internal Commitments

Today, many of us as Christian men, along with our wives, definitely consider ourselves religious. We may go to church regularly, we may have been baptized, and we may even substantially support the ministry financially. We're also committed to the basic tenets of Christianity: the deity of Christ, salvation by grace, that the Bible is the Word of God, and that Jesus Christ is coming again. But at the heart level there is something missing in many of our lives. We are more committed to the externals of the Christian faith than we are to the internal aspects, such as reflecting the fruit of the Spirit, which the apostle Paul describes as "love, joy, peace, patience, kindness, goodness, faithfulness, gentleness, and self-control" (Gal. 5:22).

Unfortunately, most of us live in a culture that is out of harmony with these Christian values. Consequently, we must constantly be on guard against the subtle influences of the world system, which the apostle John defines as "the cravings of sinful man, the lust of his eyes and the boasting of what he has and does" (1 John 2:16).

Compensation for Guilt

Frankly, I also believe many of us as Christian men perform our religious duties to compensate for our failures. We know in our hearts we are not committed to Jesus Christ as we should be. We know we're toying with sinful thoughts that dull our spiritual lives. We're playing around with the sensual aspects of a worldly lifestyle. We're making decisions in our businesses that are questionable, if not downright unethical. Our language is often not honoring to God. We give the appearance of being religious—in actuality, to compensate for our guilt.

If any of what I've just shared is true in your own life, ask God to help you practice Paul's exhortation to the Philippians: "Finally, brothers, whatever is true, whatever is noble, whatever is right, whatever is pure, whatever is lovely, whatever is admirable—if anything is excellent or praiseworthy—think about such things" (Phil. 4:8).

Principle 2. As parents, when we show favoritism in family situations, we create tensions that destroy oneness and unity.

Again and again we see this principle illustrated in the Old Testament. Isaac "loved Esau, but Rebekah loved Jacob" (Gen. 25:28). The results were devastating. When Jacob married, he "loved Rachel more than Leah" (29:30). Again, the results were disastrous. Later, Jacob "loved Joseph more than any of his other sons." Consequently, Joseph's brothers "hated him and could not speak a kind word to him" (37:3–4).

Favoritism always creates jealousy which always leads to a great deal of emotional pain. This is once again illustrated in our present study. Hannah suffered terribly because of Elkanah's favoritism.

It takes a great deal of wisdom to avoid this mistake in our families. Avoiding favoritism does not mean we shouldn't honor our children's achievements and encourage them as individuals. However, we must do so in a way that causes all of our children to feel we're being fair and impartial.

It's particularly difficult to practice this principle when some of our children are responsive to spiritual things and others are not. It's at this point we need to seek counsel from someone who has wisdom far beyond our own—a person who can help us differentiate between refusing to condone a sinful lifestyle and being fair and impartial.

Principle 3. As men particularly, we should not be threatened by our wives' emotional states but should learn to handle their mood swings with empathy, sensitivity, and understanding.

This is a difficult task for most men, as it was for Elkanah. We're basically "doers." When our wives become emotional, we want to fix the problem. Our natural tendency is to be threatened and to blame ourselves for what is happening.

Most of us as men need to develop our "listening skills." This involves getting beyond the cerebral aspects of the problem and trying to understand feelings. We must understand that most women already know intuitively what they are experiencing sometimes doesn't make sense. In fact, they may even feel guilty for being so irrational. In other words, they already know, or at least believe, they "shouldn't feel" the way they are feeling. To be told what they already have concluded only intensifies their guilt and fuels their tendency to be defensive. What they want is a sincere listening ear.

Principle 4. God responds to prayer that flows from a heart that is broken and sincere.

As I reflected on Hannah's persistent and agonizing prayer, I immediately thought of a parable that Jesus told His disciples in order "to show them that they should always pray and not give up" (Luke 18:1). It's a powerful story and speaks for itself:

> "In a certain town there was a judge who neither feared God nor cared about men. And there was a widow in that town who kept coming to him with the plea, 'Grant me justice against my adversary.'
>
> "For some time he refused. But finally he said to himself, 'Even though I don't fear God or care about men, yet because this widow keeps bothering me, I will see that she gets justice, so that she won't eventually wear me out with her coming!'"

Jesus then made the application. He said:

> "Listen to what the unjust judge says. And will not God bring about justice for his chosen ones, who cry out to him day and night? Will he keep putting them off? I tell you, he will see that they get justice, and quickly" (Luke 18:2–8a).

God *does* honor persistent prayer that comes from a broken heart, particularly when our requests are in harmony with His will. The apostle John underscored this truth in his first epistle: "This is the confidence we have in approaching God: that if we ask anything according to his will, he hears us. And if we know that he hears us—whatever we ask—we know that we have what we asked of him" (5:14–15).

Principle 5. All Christian parents should dedicate their children to the Lord, praying that they'll grow up to be committed to doing God's will in every respect.

Hannah's willingness to give her son for service in the temple as a Nazirite all the days of his life was a unique Old Testament practice. However, this religious rite yields a very important principle for Christians of all time. God wants all of us to bring up our children in "the training and instruction of the Lord" (Eph. 6:4). The place to start is with Hannah's attitude. Even before our children are born, our desire for them—male or female—should be that they come to know the Lord Jesus Christ as personal Savior and then serve Him with all their hearts—no matter what their vocation in life.

Both my wife and I have beautiful memories—not of the events themselves because we were too young—but of being told what happened.

Shortly after I was born in 1932, my mother was listening to a special church service on her little battery-operated radio back on the farm in Indiana. The speaker was Harry Ironside, the pastor of the Moody Memorial Church in Chicago. He was conducting a special dedication service and invited parents to come forward to present their children to the Lord.

This was a new experience for my mother. The religious community in which I grew up didn't have this kind of service. Furthermore, I was her firstborn.

Mom was moved by what she was hearing and so she decided to participate. She went to my crib, picked me up and then carried me into her little kitchen. There she knelt within hearing distance of what was happening 100 miles away in Chicago. That day my mother dedicated me to the Lord. I have no way of knowing what the pastor prayed, but years later when Mother told me what she had done, I understood more fully at least one reason why I had a tender heart toward God and wanted to do His will, even as a small child. I firmly believe that God answered both the pastor's prayer as well as my mother's prayer— a prayer that has impacted my life to this very day.

My wife's experience is more uniquely related to Samuel's. When her mother was in labor, she had difficulty giving birth because the umbilical cord was wrapped around Elaine's neck. In those days, this was even more dangerous than it is today. Elaine almost suffocated. When she entered this world, she had already turned deathly blue.

Being aware that she might lose her little girl as well as her own life, Elaine's mother prayed a very specific prayer—a prayer reflecting her anguish and fear. "Heavenly Father," she pleaded, " if you allow us both to live, I'll serve you the rest of my life and I'll make sure my little girl does, too."

As with me, Elaine's mother didn't share this experience with her until many years later—just shortly before she died at age 94. This was probably very wise since it might have put my wife on a guilt trip. But when she did share this story, a lot that had happened in my wife's life made more sense. Her mother's sincere prayer of dedication had made a difference in Elaine's life, and has impacted her to this very day, including the way she has reared our own children and the way she relates to our grandchildren.

Personalizing These Principles

The following questions will help you personalize these principles:

1. Do you know Christ personally, or is your Christian faith a matter of external conformity to a set of rules and regulations? And if you are a born-again Christian, have you internalized Christian truth, reflecting God's love in all of your relationships? Are you truly reflecting the fruit of the Holy Spirit and growing in your Christian life? Do you serve God out of obligation or because you love Him?

2. Do you consistently avoid showing any favoritism in your family relationships? Do you consciously think about this question and make decisions that will not violate this important biblical truth? If you have shown favoritism, what steps are you taking to correct the problem?

3. As a man, how do you handle your wife's emotional pain? Do you give her opportunity to ventilate her feelings without her feeling threatened and without trying to fix the problem? Do you do the same with your children? Have you learned to listen?

4. How do you evaluate your prayer life? Do you really share openly and honestly with the Lord what you are feeling? Do you share the desires of your heart? Are these desires in harmony with God's will? Do you believe that God really cares?

5. Have you dedicated your children to the Lord, realizing it is not too late to take this step, even if they are grown and even married? More importantly, have you dedicated your own life to the Lord? Note: If your children are grown and unable or unwilling to participate, you can still dedicate them privately.

Set a Goal

As you reflect on the principles outlined in this chapter, ask the Holy Spirit to reveal to you which one needs the most attention? Then, set a personal goal:

_____

_____

_____

_____

Memorize the Following Scripture

And this is the confidence we have in approaching God: that if we ask anything according to his will, he hears us. And if we know that he hears us—whatever we ask—we know that we have what we asked of him.

1 JOHN 5:14–15

Growing Together

The following questions are designed for small group discussion:

1. How would you define Christianity that is more external than internal?

2. Have you ever experienced the negative results that come from showing favoritism—either as the one being favored or the one being neglected? How did it impact your personal feelings and your family relationships?

3. What are some practical suggestions to help us avoid showing favoritism in our family relationships? How can we honor our children yet not reward sinful behavior?

4. What have you learned about how to handle your wife's feelings? Would you feel free to share some negative experiences as well as some positive ones?

5. Can you share an answer to prayer that has grown out of a painful and persistent prayer experience?

6. Have you ever consciously dedicated your children to the Lord? If not, why not?

7. In what way can we pray for you specifically?

Chapter 3

A Thankful Heart
Read 1 Samuel 1:21–2:10

I have a Christian friend who went through a period of deep depression. He felt so badly he had difficulty functioning on the job. When we met together and I looked into his eyes, I saw panic. His whole face appeared downcast!

This man's feelings were predictable and understandable. He gave up a very lucrative position in the business world because his Christian values conflicted with the way this particular firm did business. At the same time, he discovered his wife was having an affair, and she eventually divorced him. He was also experiencing intense guilt because he had succumbed to sexual temptation. Even though he had broken off the relationship the day we talked, and had confessed his sins and received forgiveness, his mind was still obsessed with thoughts of wanting to continue to be with this woman—a relationship he knew would never become permanent and legitimate.

As he poured out his heart to me that day, I saw a man who was deeply troubled, emotionally and spiritually. "You may be chemically depressed," I said. "You need to see both a doctor and a counselor—a doctor who can diagnose your physical condition and prescribe an appropriate antidepressant and a Christian counselor who can help you work through your deep feelings of rejection, confusion, and guilt. Furthermore," I said, "you need to start attending church on a regular basis in order to have fellowship with other Christians and to be fed the Word of God."

My friend agreed and followed through immediately. Several weeks later, if I hadn't known better, I would have thought I was talking to a different person. The twinkle I had once seen was back in his eyes. He had emerged from his "black hole." The smile on his face had returned. He was at peace with himself, his obsessive thoughts had dissipated, and he was back in church.

"No Longer Downcast"

Think for a moment how Elkanah must have felt when he saw the dramatic changes that took place in Hannah's countenance and behavior. She too had been terribly depressed—so much so that she lost her appetite and couldn't control her tears (1 Sam. 1:7). But after her encounter with Eli, she experienced a sudden change. Her "face was no longer downcast" (1:18). After years of anxiety and stress, she was at peace with both God and herself. Though Hannah may have been chemically depressed, she didn't need an anti-depressant to help her regain her emotional composure. Perhaps God miraculously healed her emotions right then and there. And certainly, Eli's reassurance helped to change her perspective on life. She knew her prayer was going to be answered. She was going to have a son (1:19–20).

A Shared Experience

Hannah was a different woman. It probably took time for Elkanah to accept what had happened—particularly to develop the same confidence in God as Hannah's. However, time proved Hannah right. She "conceived and gave birth to a son" and "named him Samuel" (1:20).

After Samuel was born, Hannah's vow must have become Elkanah's vow. We read that he went up to Shiloh annually "to fulfill *his* vow!" (1:21, emphasis mine). Was this a different vow—or was it the vow Hannah had made in the presence of the Lord and Eli? I personally believe Elkanah joined his wife, Hannah, in mind and spirit and agreed to offer Samuel to the Lord all the days of his life. As head of the household, he felt a sense of responsibility to make sure they *both* made good on this promise.

A Mother's Love

It was common in Israel for a mother to nurse a child until the age of three. Consequently, after Samuel was born, Hannah decided to stay at home during the annual sacrifices at Shiloh until her son had been weaned (1:21). Intuitively, she understood how important those first three years are in a child's life. Scientific studies have demonstrated that if children develop a sense of security during these early years, they are able to endure unusual trauma in their lives without suffering serious personality disorders.

I remember reading about a study conducted on children in England after World War II. Children who had had secure home environments during the first three years went through the bombings in London with little negative effect on their lives. Children who had grown up in insecure homes—particularly during the first three years—often developed a variety of personality disorders later in life.

One thing is certain: Samuel had a very secure home life during these first three years. He nursed at his mother's breast and felt the warmth and security of her love.

A Father's Insecurity

Though Elkanah agreed to allow Hannah to miss the annual sacrifices, it seemed he was nervous about it. "Do what seems best to you," he responded to Hannah's decision, which seems to be a concession rather than an enthusiastic response. "Stay here until you have weaned him; only may the Lord make good His word" (1:23).

This positive but somewhat hesitant response once again reflects Elkanah's religious commitments. Was he fearful that God might withhold His blessing in some way because Hannah failed to participate in the special services at Shiloh? Perhaps he was afraid that God would interpret this as hesitancy on their part to fulfill their vow. To Elkanah, a promise was a promise—a vow never to be broken.

Whatever Elkanah's feelings about the matter, he honored Hannah's decision to stay at home in order to care for her son the next three years. Frankly, it appears that Hannah's relationship with God was based more on trust and intimacy. Elkanah's relationship with the Lord seems more external and legalistic.

A Promise Fulfilled

God knew Hannah's heart. She was not reneging on her promise. Three years later she went to Shiloh, not only to offer animal and meal sacrifices to the Lord, but to offer her son as well. The scriptural record speaks for itself: "When they had slaughtered the bull, they brought the boy to Eli, and she said to him, 'As surely as you live, my lord, I am the woman who stood here beside you praying to the LORD. I prayed for this child, and the LORD has granted me what I asked of Him. So now I give him to the LORD. For his whole life he will be given over to the LORD" (1:25–28).

Becoming God's Man Today

Principles to Live By

There are three dynamic biblical principles from this wonderful story that apply to all of us today.

*Principle 1. As Christians, God wants us to make one
basic voluntary "vow" that will affect our total lifestyle—
to offer our bodies to Jesus Christ as a living sacrifice
(Rom. 12:1–2; Eph. 4:1).*

This New Testament "vow" is best summarized in Paul's letter to the Romans: "Therefore, I urge you, brothers, in view of God's mercy, to offer your bodies as living sacrifices, holy and pleasing to God—this is your spiritual act of worship. Do not conform any longer to the pattern of this world, but be transformed by the renewing of your mind. Then you will be able to test and approve what God's will is—his good, pleasing and perfect will" (12:1–2).

Note that Paul "urges" all Christians to respond *willingly* to God. His appeal is based on God's mercy and grace. Though we certainly have a spiritual and moral obligation to live in His will because of all God has done for us in Christ Jesus, He wants our willing and grateful act of love. Just as every husband wants a godly wife who submits out of appreciation for his sacrificial love, so Christ wants us—His bride— to willingly submit to His will out of deep appreciation and love for His death on the cross to pay for our sins so that we might have eternal life.

*Principle 2. As Christians, we should be motivated by God's
grace to keep our vow to the Lord—not by the laws of the
Old Testament.*

This principle is best illustrated in Paul's letter to Titus, when he wrote: "For the *grace of God* that brings salvation has appeared to all men. *It teaches us* to say 'No' to ungodliness and worldly passions, and to live self-controlled, upright and godly lives in this present age, while we wait for the blessed hope— the glorious appearing of our great God and Savior, Jesus Christ, who gave himself for us to redeem us from all wickedness and to purify for himself a people that are his very own, *eager to do what is good"* (Titus 2:11–14, emphasis mine).

This great New Testament principle is simply an extension of the first principle—that God's mercy and love should motivate us to present our bodies to Jesus Christ as living sacrifices that are not conformed to the world. God wants us to respond to His unmerited favor—His grace—not His laws that *demand* our allegiance.

When we understand this great truth, we also understand that when we violate His will, we are deliberately turning our back on the Savior of the world who gave everything to redeem us from eternal damnation. To do so is the ultimate in ungratefulness, which leads to the next principle.

Principle 3. As Christians, we must be on guard against the temptation to take advantage of God's grace, living carnal rather than spiritual lives that reflect the fruit of the Spirit.

When we deliberately take God's grace for granted, we are demonstrating an ungrateful attitude that cannot be described in human terms. There is no earthly illustration that even comes close to explaining what it means for a Christian to ignore God's gift of salvation.

Consider the marital partner who turns his back on a faithful mate, ignoring his wedding vows and committing adultery. Today many men divorce their wives as they grow older and marry "trophy wives"—younger women who make them feel good and enhance their image in the business world. Without a twinge of conscience, they forget the years their first wives have sacrificed to bear children, to rear those children, and to care faithfully for the home.

Consider other human beings who lose their lives by stepping in front of a speeding train or bullet to save another person's life. The recipient of that grace then totally forgets what it cost another person to save his life. During the very week I was reflecting on this principle, two men actually lost their lives while trying to save a young girl who fell in front of a train. Though injured, she was pushed to safety while her saviors were killed. I wonder how long it will take for this young woman—even with constant reminders—to virtually forget this incredible event.

These illustrations fall short of explaining what we do when we take advantage of God's grace and ignore His greatest gift—the gift of His only begotten Son.

Imagine how God the Father feels when we ignore His love. The major reason He saved us is to be redeemed people who "are eager to do what is good." Imagine how sad it makes the Son of God when we fail to conform our lives to His image after He suffered and died that we might live forever. And imagine how we must grieve the Holy Spirit when we follow "the acts of the sinful nature" rather than manifesting the fruit of the Holy Spirit (Gal. 5:19–23).

Personalizing These Principles

The following questions are designed to help you personalize these principles. As you read, ask the Holy Spirit to reveal any areas of your life that needs special attention.

1. As a Christian, in view of all God has done for you in sending His Son to die for you in order that you might be saved, have you presented your body to Christ as a living sacrifice? Has there been a point in your life when you told God you're giving your total being to Him because of what He has done for you? If not, why not?

2. As a Christian, why are you serving Jesus Christ? Are you motivated to live a holy and righteous life, not because God demands it, but because you are overwhelmed by His grace in saving you from eternal damnation?

3. As a Christian, are you taking advantage of God's love and grace by making decisions that are definitely out of His will and simply assuming that His blood will continue to cleanse you from your sins?

Set a Goal

As you reflect on the principles outlined in this chapter and the questions you've just read, ask the Holy Spirit to reveal to you the principle in your life that needs the most attention. Once you've made a decision, set a personal goal:

_____

_____

_____

Memorize the Following Scripture

Therefore, I urge you, brothers, in view of God's mercy, to offer your bodies as living sacrifices, holy and pleasing to God—this is your spiritual act of worship. Do not conform any longer to the pattern of this world, but be transformed by the renewing of your mind.

ROMANS 12:1–2

Growing Together

The following questions are designed for small group discussion:

1. Why do some Christians refuse to offer their bodies to Jesus Christ as a living sacrifice? If you've struggled—or are struggling—with this decision, would you share the reason or reasons why?

2. Why do some Christians try to serve God because of legalistic demands rather than because they're thankful for all that God has done for them? Has this ever happened in your life? How did this affect your motivation when you understood "grace" rather than "law"?

3. In what ways do Christians take advantage of God's grace? Can you share an experience in which you have personally taken advantage of God's grace?

4. In what way can we pray for you personally?

Chapter 4

The Priority of Praise
Read 1 Samuel 2:1–10

*A*ngeles Silesius once wrote—

> Man has two eyes.
> One only sees what happens in fleeting time,
> The other what is eternal and divine![1]

The man who penned these words probably didn't understand the implications of what he wrote as it applies to statements in Holy Scripture. However, this bit of prose certainly describes what often happens supernaturally when Bible personalities were touched by the Holy Spirit and uttered words that were both human and divine.

This happened to Hannah when she gave birth to Samuel. As you read her prayer of praise, did you notice that she not only reflected her present victory over Peninnah and her own barrenness, but she also spoke words that were directly related to the history of Israel and the promised Messiah. They are prophetic statements that affect us all. Hannah "discerned in her own individual experience the general laws of the divine economy and its significance in relationship to the whole history to the kingdom of God."[2]

Let's look more carefully at Hannah's prayer of praise, attempting to see beyond the immediate events that inspired her to pen one of the most beautiful and perceptive prayers recorded in the Bible.

A Prayer of Deliverance

Hannah praised God for delivering her from her barren condition. We read: "My heart rejoices *in the LORD; in the LORD* my horn is lifted high" (1 Sam. 2:1a).

"In the Lord"

The key phrase in this proclamation of praise—which Hannah repeats—is "in the LORD." Hannah did not rejoice because of her own achievement as a mother. She was acknowledging that her little boy was a miracle child. In her despair, she had "poured out" her "soul *to the Lord*" (1:15; emphasis mine). Mercifully, God had answered her prayer. She had tried again and again to get pregnant, but "the Lord had closed her womb" (1:5).

Then it happened! When Eli blessed her with the words, "Go in peace, and may the God of Israel grant you what you have asked of Him" (1:17), Hannah knew that God was going to have mercy and answer the sincere prayer that flowed from her broken and contrite heart. Her depression subsided and her downcast face reflected a calm and settled peace (1:18).

When Samuel was born, Hannah wanted everyone to know that this little boy was a gift from God—not the product of her own achievement and her own strength. Consequently, she proclaimed—*In the Lord*, my horn is lifted high" (2:1a, emphasis mine).

In Old Testament poetic literature, the writers used the word "horn" or "horns" to symbolized strength. For example, when Moses blessed the tribes of Israel and paid tribute to Joseph, he wrote: "In majesty he is like a firstborn bull; his horns are the horns of a wild ox. With them he will gore the nations, even those at the ends of the earth" (Deut. 33:17).

By using this metaphor—a "bull" or "wild ox"—it may appear that Moses was paying tribute to Joseph's own strength —his power, his ability to subdue nations, his personal wisdom and discernment. But Moses had learned too much about reliance on God to make such a statement. Of all men, Moses understood that without God's empowerment, we are like dust. Before he raised his staff in the air and stretched out his hand over the Red Sea, he cried out to the people: "Do not be afraid. Stand firm and you will see the deliverance the LORD will bring you today" (Exod. 14:13).

The Lord's Deliverance

In a moment of divine inspiration, Hannah understood this great truth. She wanted the whole world to know that her victory—symbolized by her "uplifted head and horn"—only pointed to the God who had delivered her from her barren condition. She took no credit for herself, which is clear when she said: "'My mouth boasts over my enemies, for I delight in *your deliverance*'" (1 Sam. 2:1b).

Hannah's next statement only underscores the desire she had to honor and praise God for delivering her from her unhappy condition. It may appear she was claiming credit for her victory over Peninnah by strutting about arrogantly with her "horn" lifted high. In actuality, she was "boasting" in the Lord. She was rejoicing in God's deliverance!

Years later, another Old Testament poet named Asaph captured what Hannah felt in her heart:

> We give thanks to you, O God,
>> we give thanks, for your Name is near;
>> men tell of your wonderful deeds.
> You say, "I choose the appointed time;
>> it is I who judge uprightly.
> When the earth and all its people quake,
>> it is I who hold its pillars firm.
> To the arrogant I say, 'Boast no more,'
>> and to the wicked, *'Do not lift up your horns.*
> *Do not lift your horns* against heaven;

do not speak with outstretched neck'"
(Ps. 75:1–5, emphasis mine).

Hannah was not lifting up her horn against heaven, nor was she boasting in herself. She was not prancing about with an outstretched neck, bragging about her victory over Peninnah, even though this woman had become an enemy who had provoked her, shamed her, and taunted her for years. Rather, Hannah was praising God for her victory "in the LORD." With head held high, she was giving glory to God!

A Prayer Focused on God's Holiness

Hannah had a new perspective on God's holiness as the one true God. She prayed: "There is no one holy like the Lord; there is no one besides you; there is no Rock like our God" (1 Sam. 2:2).

Hannah's prayer in Shiloh and God's answer deepened her conviction that the Lord was the one true God—the God of righteousness and holiness. All of the other so-called "gods" of Canaan were false—simply idols of wood or stone that could not hear or respond. When Israel worshiped these gods, it only gave birth to all kinds of wickedness and evil. Rather than giving life, they required life—even child sacrifice.

As Hannah sat holding little Samuel in her arms, nursing him at her breast, she saw true innocence and purity—a little life untouched from the pollution of the world. Samuel was a reflection of God's holy nature. The same is true of every child that is born into this world today. Though each of us has a sin nature at birth, until the imprint of a sin-sick world impacts a newborn, we see the image of God as in no other created being (Rom. 1:20).

Later in Israel's history, David composed a song of praise and used the same metaphors as Hannah to describe the Lord: "The Lord is my rock, my fortress and my deliverer; my God is my rock, in whom I take refuge, my shield and the horn of my salvation" (2 Sam. 22:2–3).

David's prayer extolled his victories over the Philistines. However, Hannah's song of praise was far more intimate and personal. For years she had been on an emotional and spiritual roller coaster. Depression had gripped her heart and soul. Even the bright moments, when Elkanah honored her with "double portions," were quickly followed by despair. Peninnah doubled her efforts at making her miserable. But now she had her feet planted firmly on the "rock of ages." She felt secure and loved—not just by Elkanah—but by God Himself.

A Prayer Extolling Humility

Hannah had learned a great lesson regarding pride versus humility. Turning her thoughts toward her fellow Israelites, she warned: "Do not keep talking so *proudly* or let your mouth speak such *arrogance*, the LORD is a God who knows, and by him deeds are weighed" (1 Sam. 2:3–5).

At this point in her prayer, the Holy Spirit enabled Hannah to broaden and deepen her perspective, to see beyond her immediate experience. Certainly Peninnah's prideful taunting over the years precipitated her thoughts at this moment, but only momentarily. The Holy Spirit reminded her that Israel's history had been filled with prideful episodes, periods of time where her fathers and forefathers had taken credit for their victories and for the possessions they had inherited in the land of Canaan.

A Miraculous Victory

Hannah's next statement may reflect the story of Gideon, a man God had used in an unusual way to demonstrate that He can give victory against impossible odds. Listen to her words: "The bows of the warriors are broken, but those who stumbled are armed with strength" (2:4).

Like so many in Israel, Gideon's father, Joash, had forsaken the one true God, and His judgment once again fell on the children of Israel. We're told that "Midian so impoverished the Israelites that they cried out to the LORD for help" (Judg. 6:6). And once again, God in His mercy responded to their plea for deliverance. He chose Gideon, Joash's son, to communicate to Israel His power and greatness.

Understandably, Gideon was skeptical when an angel of the Lord appeared to him. However, God reassured him by saying, "Go in the strength you have and save Israel out of Midian's hand. Am I not sending you?" (6:14).

Gideon responded to God's call on his life and assembled thousands of men to attack the Midianites. However, the Lord did something very strange. He told Gideon to reduce his army. From a human point of view, this was anything but a rational maneuver. But God made it clear why He wanted to use this strategy: "In order that Israel may not boast against me that her own strength has saved her, announce now to the people, 'Anyone who trembles with fear may turn back and leave Mount Gilead.' So twenty-two thousand men left, while ten thousand remained" (7:2–3).

Gideon's Three Hundred Men

You can imagine Gideon's amazement when the Lord told him to reduce his army even further. Only those men who drank water by cupping their hands were to go with him. This reduced Gideon's army to only three hundred men (7:6). Imagine this young man's response when God told him he would deliver Israel with this small contingency of Israelites.

It's not unrealistic to conclude that the Holy Spirit may have brought Gideon's victory to Hannah's mind as she was praising God. More specifically, she may have thought of what happened to the Midianite warriors who were armed with bows and arrows and spears. Gideon divided his small contingency into three groups—one hundred in each battalion. He then "placed trumpets and empty jars in the hands of all of them, with torches inside" (7:16). These men then entered the camp of this well-armed militia that was as "thick as locusts" (7:12). When they blew their trumpets in the midst of the enemy camp and broke their empty jars with torches inside, they created such consternation that the enemy warriors attacked each other. The Midianites defeated themselves. God had devised this simple plan to demonstrate to Israel that they could not save themselves in their own strength" (7:2).

Against the backdrop of this great victory, note again the words of Hannah in her prayer of praise: "'The bows of the warriors are broken, but those who stumbled are armed with strength'" (1 Sam. 2:4).

Hannah's prayer certainly refers to far more than her victory over Peninnah. Through her, the Holy Spirit was giving a message to all Israel—and to us. If we place our confidence in ourselves and forget the Lord, we are headed for defeat and disaster. On the other hand, if we follow God faithfully, even if we're in the minority, we can defeat our enemies.

Poverty and Plenty

Hannah used another illustration to demonstrate what happens when we put our confidence in ourselves and forsake the Lord: "Those who were full hire themselves out for food, but those who were hungry hunger no more" (1 Sam. 2:5a).

This illustration is both historical and prophetic. From a historical perspective it describes Israel's plight again and again. When God's people inherited the land and lacked nothing (Deut. 8:9), they became proud and took credit for what they had accumulated (8:14). They ignored Moses' warning when he said: "Be careful that you do not forget the LORD your God, failing to observe his commands, his laws and his decrees that I am giving you this day. Otherwise, when you eat and are satisfied, when you build fine houses and settle down, and when your herds and flocks grow large and your silver and gold increase and all you have is multiplied, then your heart will become proud and you will forget the LORD your God, who brought you out of Egypt, out of the land of slavery" (Deut. 8:11–14).

Sadly, Israel forgot this warning again and again and ended up in slavery. "Those who were full" had to "hire themselves out for food." But those who repented and trusted God no longer were hungry. God took care of them (1 Sam. 2:5).

A Fruitful Vine

Hannah's final illustration definitely refers to herself, but again it has a much broader meaning: "She who was barren has borne seven children, but she who has had many sons pines away" (2:5b).

At this point, Hannah was clearly referring to her rival, Peninnah. Later we read that "the LORD was gracious to Hannah; she conceived and gave birth to three sons and two daughters"—a total of five (2:21). It appears that while Hannah became "like a fruitful vine" (Ps. 128:3), Peninnah became barren.

But note that Hannah refers to the fact that the one who "was barren has borne seven children." Why this disparity? What is the Holy Spirit saying through Hannah's lips? Most Bible commentators believe that the number seven symbolizes perfection—which takes us back to the "blessings" and the "curses" reiterated by Moses when he had reviewed the law of God before Israel entered the land of Canaan. If Israel obeyed the laws of God, the fruit of their womb would be blessed (Deut. 28:4). If they disobeyed God, the fruit of their womb would be cursed (28:18).

Once again, Hannah's prayer of praise gives us a perspective on God's great plan for Israel. Her experience in giving birth to Samuel illustrates what will happen if God's people follow His perfect will and obey, as well as what will happen if they walk out of His will and disobey.

A Prayer Reflecting God's Sovereignty

Hannah developed a whole new perspective on God's power. At this point, her prayer broadens considerably and focuses on God's sovereign control over His total creation and why it is so important that we follow Him fully. If we do not, we will suffer the consequences. Hannah's words speak for themselves:

- "The LORD brings death and makes alive; he brings down to the grave and raises up."
- "The LORD sends poverty and wealth; he humbles and he exalts."
- "He raises the poor from the dust and lifts the needy from the ash heap; he seats them with princes and has them inherit a throne of honor."

"For the foundations of the earth are the LORD's; upon them he has set the world. He will guard the feet of his saints, but the wicked will be silenced in darkness. It is not by strength that one prevails; those who oppose the LORD will be shattered. He will thunder against them from heaven; the LORD will judge the ends of the earth." (1 Sam. 2:6–10a)

A Prophetic Prayer

In her time of prayer and praise, Hannah caught a glimpse of the coming Messiah. Limited in understanding, she cried out: "'He will give strength to his king and exalt the horn of his anointed'" (2:10b).

Hannah certainly didn't understand what we now know regarding God's promise to Abraham—that the nation born in Sarah's womb would eventually give birth to the Messiah to be the Savior of the world (Gen. 12:2–3). However, the Holy Spirit enlightened her heart to see in her own experience a glimpse of this great future event.

What happened to Hannah is also a beautiful picture of what would eventually happen to a young girl named Mary. There's a unique similarity but also a great difference in these two experiences. Both Hannah and Mary conceived miraculously. But the father of Jesus was God Himself. Even so, when you compare Hannah's prayer of praise with Mary's following her divine pregnancy, you'll see some remarkable similarities (Luke 1:46–55).

Becoming God's Man Today

Principles to Live By

As men, what can we learn from Hannah's prayer of praise? Following are some powerful principles that the Holy Spirit wants to use to penetrate our lives.

Principle 1. God will exalt those who are humble and will humble those who exalt themselves.

Biblical writers from Genesis to Revelation emphasize the importance of humility and the dangers of pride. For example, listen to a classic passage from the apostle Paul's letter to the Philippians:

> Do nothing out of selfish ambition or vain conceit, but in humility consider others better than yourselves. Each of you should look not only to your own interests, but also to the interests of others. Your attitude should be the same as that of Christ Jesus:
>
> > Who, being in very nature God,
> > > did not consider equality with God
> > > > something to be grasped,
> > but made himself nothing,
> > > taking the very nature of a servant,
> > > being made in human likeness.

And being found in appearance as a man,
    he humbled himself
    and became obedient to death—
        even death on a cross. (Phil. 2:3–8)

A Haughty Spirit Before a Fall

One of the most vivid illustrations of how pride comes before a fall hit the city of Dallas during the NFL football season in 1995. Jerry Jones, the primary owner of the Dallas Cowboys, had just paid millions of dollars to entice Deion Sanders away from the San Francisco 49ers. Shortly after Deion joined the team, Dallas hosted the 49ers at Texas Stadium. Already leading the NFL in victories, the media was predicting a blow-out—a humiliating defeat for San Francisco—especially since their star quarterback was injured.

At the same time, Jerry Jones—who by his own admission is not noted for humility—had participated in preparing a special television ad featuring the exploits of Deion Sanders. In the same ad, Jones is super-imposed over Deion shouting—"If I had eleven men like Deion, I could rule the world!"

Ironically, at the time this ad was running on national television during the game, the 49ers were giving the Cowboys a humiliating defeat! As I watched this game, I couldn't help but think of the principle of Scripture stated so succinctly in the book of Proverbs: "Pride goes before destruction, a haughty spirit before a fall" (Prov. 16:18).

"Meekness Is Not Weakness"

When we discuss humility, it's important to understand that meekness does not mean weakness. It's not sinful to have self-confidence. It's not wrong to believe in ourselves. It's not inappropriate to tackle problems with the attitude that we know we can do certain things. Athletes who don't believe in their capabilities are headed for defeat.

When David went out to meet Goliath, he had great confidence in his skill with a slingshot. Some believe he selected five stones, not because he was afraid he'd miss with the first one, but because Goliath had four brothers who might come to Goliath's rescue. But whatever was in David's mind, he knew he was a talented young man. He'd spent hours and days on the hillsides of Judea watching his father's flocks and at the same time practicing the use of his slingshot. He had honed this skill, probably like the seven hundred left-handed men from Gibeah who could "sling a stone at a hair and not miss" (Judg. 20:16).

As David went out to meet Goliath, it's obvious he had self-confidence. But, he beautifully blended his self-confidence with his confidence in God. Listen to his words, which speak for themselves: "David said to the Philistine, 'You come against me with sword and spear and javelin, but I come against you in the name of the LORD Almighty, the God of the armies of Israel, whom you have defied. This day the LORD will hand you over to me, and I'll strike you down . . . . All those gathered here will know that it is not by sword or spear that the LORD saves; for the battle is the LORD's, and he will give all of you into our hands'" (1 Sam. 17:45–47).

And so it is today. We need to use every talent God has given us and develop our skills the best we can. We need to be diligent and committed to excellence. But undergirding, surrounding, and permeating everything we do should be an attitude of trust in the Almighty God. We must understand that if we proceed believing that we are the source of our accomplishments, we'll eventually fail miserably. God will not tolerate pride indefinitely. The fall will come and probably when we least expect it.

Principle 2. As Christians, we must fight our spiritual battles in God's strength, believing we can be victorious when we put on the full armor of God.

David cried out to Goliath that "the battle is the LORD's!" This is particularly true as we face our greatest enemy, Satan himself. It's dangerous to attempt to win physical battles in our own strength! But it's lethal to attempt to win spiritual battles on our own. This is why Paul exhorted the Ephesian believers to "be strong in the Lord and in his mighty power" and to "put on the full armor of God" so that they could take their "stand against the devil's schemes" (Eph. 6:10–11). Again, it's one thing to struggle "against flesh and blood," but it is yet another thing to take on the forces of evil in this world.

In a metaphorical but a powerful way Paul outlines how to defeat Satan:

Stand firm then,
- with the belt of truth buckled around your waist,
- with the breastplate of righteousness in place, and
- with your feet fitted with the readiness that comes from the gospel of peace.

In addition to all this,
- take up the shield of faith, with which you can extinguish all the flaming arrows of the evil one.
- Take the helmet of salvation and the sword of the Spirit, which is the word of God.
- And pray in the Spirit on all occasions with all kinds of prayers and requests.

With this in mind,
- be alert and always keep on praying for all the saints (Eph. 6:14–18).

Principle 3. As Christians, we must not fail to worship God— to thank and praise Him: first, for His glorious gift of salvation, and second, for all the blessings of life.

Hannah did not fail to remember what God had done for her. How easy it would have been to get caught up in her own gratification and to use this experience as an opportunity to glorify herself. After all, she had spent years being humiliated by Peninnah. But rather than focusing on herself, she focused on God.

Today, many of us fail to thank and praise God for the blessings of life. We sit down at tables laden with food and never say "thank you" to the One who has provided it. We build our homes and live in them from day to day without praising God for the resources to construct them. We live in a country where we have tremendous freedoms—and yet we take these liberties for granted and do not thank God on a regular basis for the privilege. We make money, we spend it, and we save it without giving God our first fruits—which I personally believe ought to be at least a tithe or ten percent. And frankly, I believe God should get His share before the government gets its share—in other words, I believe in tithing on my gross salary—not after taxes.

We must remember as Christians that giving our material possessions should always be an act of praise and worship. And to withhold our gifts is an act of selfishness, pride, and arrogance. We are definitely taking advantage of the grace of God.

And a final lesson from Hannah is that we often take our precious children and grandchildren for granted. Every day we should thank God and praise Him for new life that comes into this world. How tragic that we live in a society where babies are legally aborted, murdered, and destroyed by the millions. May God have mercy on our nation! To take the life of unborn children is one of the greatest acts of selfishness, pride, and arrogance that exists in our society. We have put ourselves in the place of God. How dare we destroy life that He creates! Sadly, we do it every minute of every day.

Personalizing These Principles

Read the following Scriptures and evaluate your life. To what extent are you following God's standard of righteousness?

Principle 1:

All of you, clothe yourselves with humility toward one another, because, "God opposes the proud but gives grace to the humble." Humble yourselves, therefore, under God's mighty hand, that he may lift you up in due time (1 Pet. 5:5–6).

Principle 2:

Now to him who is able to do immeasurably more than all we ask or imagine, according to his power that is at work within us, to him be glory in the church and in Christ Jesus throughout all generations, for ever and ever! Amen (Eph. 3:20–21).

Principle 3:

Oh, the depth of the riches of the wisdom and knowledge of God! How unsearchable his judgments and his paths beyond tracing out! "Who has known the mind of the Lord? Or who has been his counselor?" "Who has ever given to God, that God should repay him?" For from him and through him and to him are all things. To him be the glory forever! Amen (Rom. 11:33–36).

Set a Goal

As you reflect on the principles outlined in this chapter, which one needs the most attention? Is it your tendency to be prideful? Are you trying to fight spiritual battles in your own strength? To what extent are you really worshiping and praising God for all that He's done for you? Once you've asked the Holy Spirit to help you determine your greatest need, set a personal goal:

_____

_____

_____

_____

Memorize the Following Scripture

There is no one holy like the LORD; there is no one besides you; there is no Rock like our God

1 SAMUEL 2:2.

Growing Together

The following questions are designed for small group discussion:

1. In what ways have you seen God humble people who exalt themselves? Has this ever happened to you? Feel free to share your personal experience.

2. When did you last try to fight a spiritual battle in your own strength? What happened? What did you learn from this experience?

3. How would you define a true worship experience? How do you feel when you're having this kind of experience? What factors create this kind of experience in your life?

4. In what way can we pray for you personally?

Chapter 5

Wickedness in High Places
Read 1 Samuel 2:12–36

*T*he week I began writing this chapter, the President of the United States was once again in the news as an object of continuing investigation for unethical behavior. At the same time, the Speaker of the House, representing the opposing political party, was being investigated by the House Ethics Committee for inappropriate behavior related to the tax laws of the United States. And anyone who has followed the sad saga of Prince Charles and Princess Diana in England is well aware of their admitted extramarital affairs and subsequent divorce.

The business world is another arena where scandals have made international news. Prominent businessmen—some who claim to be Christians—are in prison serving sentences for engaging in unlawful business practices. The savings and loan fiasco was a frightening example of the way some people do business and violate standard business practices.

Unfortunately this kind of behavior is not limited to politics and business. It has also permeated the religious community. Priests have been publicly charged with the horrible crime of sexually abusing children. Prominent television evangelists and other well-known religious leaders have been charged with both immoral and unethical behavior.

Never before in the history of our own culture have we experienced so much "wickedness in high places." But the Bible makes it clear that this is nothing new, even among

God's chosen people, the children of Israel. The Bible in no way whitewashes and covers up these scandalous sins. God exposes them for the whole world to see.

"Eli's Sons Were Wicked Men"

Eli served both as a judge and as high priest in Israel and he had two sons named Hophni and Phinehas. We first meet these men in the opening verses of the book of 1 Samuel, where they are also identified as "priests of the Lord" (1:3).

Sadly, these two men did not measure up to the spiritual qualifications that God had established for spiritual leaders (Lev. 21:1–15). Rather than living righteous and holy lives, they were very "wicked" (1 Sam. 2:12a).

"No Regard for the Lord"

This phrase, "they had no regard for the LORD," can also be translated, "they knew not the LORD." Even though Eli's sons had not turned from God to worship the false gods of Canaan, they did not know God personally. Even though they were involved in a religious profession as priests in the Tabernacle at Shiloh, they were not true followers of the Lord.

When Paul addressed the Jews in his epistle to the Romans, he made it clear that there are Jews who are "believing Jews" and those who are not. More specifically, Paul said: "A man is not a Jew if he is only one outwardly, nor is circumcision merely outward and physical. No, a man is a Jew if he is one inwardly; and circumcision is circumcision of the heart, by the Spirit, not by the written code. Such a man's praise is not from men, but from God" (Rom. 2:28–29).

Eli's sons were not true Jews by God's definition. They were no doubt circumcised according to the law of Moses, but they had cold and calloused hearts. Their wickedness is almost incomprehensible.

"Treating the Lord's Offering with Contempt"

Moses had clearly outlined God's plan for the priests (Lev. 7:30–34). They were not to take the fat portions of the meat that was being offered. They were legally allowed to have the "breast" and the "right thigh," but only after the fat portions of the sacrifice had been burned upon the altar. Instead, Eli's sons had set up their own rules in order to get the best meat while the sacrifice was being boiled (1 Sam. 2:13–14).

But they took another step out of the will of God. We read that "even before the fat was burned, the servant of the priest would come and say to the man who was sacrificing, 'give the priest some meat to roast; he won't accept boiled meat from you, but only raw" (2:15). And, if anyone resisted, the servant would "take it by force" (2:16).

"Robbing God!"

God was very displeased with Eli's sons. God viewed their actions as taking for themselves what belonged to Him. As Keil & Delitzsch state: "To take the flesh of the sacrificial animal and roast it before the offering had been made, was a crime which was equivalent to a robbery of God."[1]

But more so, these men "were treating the LORD's offering with contempt." Not only were they taking from God what belonged to Him, but they were keeping people from offering sacrifices to atone for their sins. Consequently, what they did affected all Israel. They were treating "with contempt" what God had established as a means of having fellowship with His people and a way in which His people could have fellowship with Him.

"Just Suppose!"

Though I cannot think of any contemporary illustration to describe the gravity of the sin Eli's sons committed, let me share one idea that may help. The church I serve has seventeen paid pastors. Suppose we ordered our secretaries to meet our people at the door on Sunday mornings and demand they give directly to the pastors the money they had planned to give to the Lord. Though what a person gives to the Lord financially has nothing to do with the forgiveness of sins, we would certainly be taking from God what belongs to Him and hindering our people from worshiping God. Though the Lord has given us biblical guidelines specifying that pastors should be paid from the offerings of the people (1 Tim. 5:17–18; Gal. 6:6), those salaries should be paid from a portion of the offerings *after* the money has been first and foremost given to God.

Although this illustration certainly misses the mark in describing the sin committed by Hophni and Phinehas, if you multiply many times the seriousness of what I have described, you will perhaps understand a little bit of how their behavior grieved God. Sadly, some people who claim to be servants of God today are taking money people believe they are giving to God, and these individuals in turn squander it on themselves. This too is "treating the LORD's offering with contempt."

"Samuel Grew Up in the Presence of the Lord"

In spite of the terrible wickedness and outright hypocrisy that existed in the tabernacle at Shiloh, Samuel continued his spiritual journey. Eli served as his mentor, even though his own sons were woefully wicked. As a young lad, he actually performed spiritual tasks alongside Hophni and Phinehas— "ministering before the LORD" (1 Sam. 2:18). Once a year when his parents traveled to Shiloh to worship, Hannah brought him a "little robe" she had made—obviously a bit larger each year to fit his growing body. And each year, Eli pronounced a blessing on Elkanah and Hannah, asking the Lord to give them more children to replace Samuel.

God responded to Eli's prayer and blessed Hannah with "three sons and two daughters." Meanwhile, we read, "The boy Samuel grew up in the presence of the LORD" (2:21). In some miraculous way, God protected young Samuel from being negatively influenced by the corruption that existed in the house of the Lord. I'm confident Hannah must have made this issue a part of her daily prayers.

"Why Do You Do Such Things?"

"Treating the Lord's offering with contempt" was not the only sin committed by Eli's wicked sons. They were also horribly immoral—committing ritualistic fornication "with the women who served at the entrance to the Tent of Meeting" (2:22). Though Hophni and Phinehas had not forsaken the God of Abraham, Isaac, and Jacob, they had synchronized immoral Canaanite worship practices into the sacred plan God had given at Mount Sinai. In essence, they were doing what the children of Israel did when Aaron molded a golden calf. Paul warned against this evil when he wrote to the Corinthians and said, referring to the children of Israel at that moment in their lives, "Do not be idolaters, as some of them were; as it is written: 'The people sat down to eat and drink and got up to indulge in pagan revelry.' We should not commit sexual immorality, as some of them did—and in one day twenty-three thousand of them died" (1 Cor. 10:7–8).

The immorality committed by Hophni and Phinehas at Shiloh was an open scandal. Everyone knew about it—including Eli. Understandably, he was very disturbed and questioned them: "'Why do you do such things? I hear from all the people about these wicked deeds of yours. No, my sons; it is not a good report that I hear spreading among the Lord's people'" (1 Sam. 2:23–24).

Eli issued a stern warning. He made it clear that there was no who could intercede for them before God. What they had done and were continuing to do was an offense—not just against their fellow Israelites—but against Almighty God.

Sadly, Hophni and Phinehas did not listen to their father. In fact, they had gone so far down the road and had hardened their hearts so desperately that God's judgment had already been pronounced on their lives. The most foreboding words we can ever read are as follows: "It was the LORD's will to put them to death" (2:25).

Does this mean that God would not have "changed His mind" had they truly repented? Only God can answer that question. We do know that "the Lord relented" on a previous occasion when He threatened to destroy the children of Israel when they had worshiped the golden calf. How a sovereign God can change His mind is a question only He can answer. The fact is, Hophni and Phinehas did not repent. Futhermore, there was no Moses to intercede for them as he had done for the children of Israel at Mount Sinai.

The amazing and encouraging thing is that in spite of all this evil that existed in Shiloh, we read that "the boy Samuel continued to grow in stature and in favor with the Lord and with men" (2:26). Though Eli's sons did not listen to their father's warnings, evidently Samuel did. Samuel grew up to be a man who followed God in spite of his horrible environment!

"Why Do You Honor Your Sons More than Me?"

God finally ran out of patience with Eli. The Lord sent an unnamed prophet to pronounce judgment on his household. Though Eli had warned his sons, he hadn't gone far enough. Though he attempted to be a godly man himself, he didn't get beyond showing favoritism and allowing Hophni and Phinehas to continue to sin against God. As Merrill Unger points out, "Eli let his paternal love run away with his judgment; his fondness for his sons restrained him from the exercise of proper parental authority."[2]

The Lord made it clear that He considered Eli's behavior as an act of honoring his sons more than honoring God Himself

(2:29). This, of course, is an act of idolatry. How tragic it was for the high priest in Israel to fall prey to this kind of sin! But this created an even more tragic situation for both his sons and his future descendants.

"A man of God" who came to Eli delivered a painful message to this old priest: "'The time is coming when I will cut short your strength and the strength of your father's house, so that there will not be an old man in your family line and you will see distress in my dwelling. Although good will be done to Israel, in your family line there will never be an old man. Every one of you that I do not cut off from my altar will be spared only to blind your eyes with tears and to grieve your heart, and all your descendants will die in the prime of life'" (2:31–33).

This unnamed man of God also told Eli that he would receive a sign that would verify that this prophecy would come true. Both of his sons would "die on the same day" (2:34)—which indeed happened (4:11). Furthermore, the Lord would replace Eli with "a faithful priest"—a man who would walk in God's will. This godly man would be Samuel, who would serve as both judge and high priest.

As so often happens in Scripture, this prophecy has a much broader meaning and far-reaching reality. Eventually, Jesus Christ, the Messiah, would appear and become the great high priest who would serve as mediator for all who put their faith in His death and resurrection. He would become "a priest forever, in the order of Melchizedek" (Heb. 7:17).

The author of Hebrews goes on to explain it further: "Such a high priest meets our need—one who is holy, blameless, pure, set apart from sinners, exalted above the heavens. Unlike the other high priests, he does not need to offer sacrifices day after day, first for his own sins, and then for the sins of the people. He sacrificed for their sins once for all when he offered himself. For the law appoints as high priests men who are weak; but the oath, which came after the law, appointed the Son, who has been made perfect forever" (7:26–28).

Becoming God's Man Today

Principles to Live By

Following are three dynamic principles that emerge from this story. They represent both words of warning as well as words of encouragement.

Principle 1. God still uses imperfect Christians, but sin in our lives leads to serious consequences.

God used Eli even though he at times disobeyed the Word of the Lord and today God may even use us when we deliberately disobey Him. He honors His Word. But ultimately we'll pay a serious price for our sins. We will eventually reap what we sow (Gal. 6:7).

I know of a former pastor who built a very successful church. Hundreds of people professed faith in Christ under his preaching and teaching ministry. At the same time, he was living an immoral life. He had multiple affairs. But eventually his "house of cards" came crashing down. Unfortunately, his efforts at repentance were superficial, dishonest, and manipulative. Eventually, he lost his church, his marriage, and his family as well as his health. He died a relatively young man.

Don't misunderstand. Not all crises of this nature are the result of sin. But in this pastor's case—as in Eli's—the cause-effect relationship seems quite clear. This man violated God's will again and again over a lengthy period of time. It shouldn't surprise us that bad things happened since God promises He will discipline His children who continue to sin. In Corinth, some church members' sins were so flagrant that God allowed them to become terribly ill and some of them actually died. In other words, God took them home to heaven (1 Cor. 11:30).

Principle 2. God will ultimately discipline people who use religious positions to further their own selfish and sinful purposes.

There is a distinct relationship between this principle and the one we just looked at. Those of us who are actually in the ministry will experience greater discipline if we take advantage of God's people.

Paul also underscored this principle when he wrote to the Corinthians. As an apostle, he had "laid a foundation as an expert builder." He went on to say that others were building on this foundation, which was Jesus Christ. He warned everyone that he should be careful how he builds on this foundation (1 Cor. 3:10–13).

Paul then issued an awesome warning. "Don't you know," he wrote, "that you yourselves are God's temple"—that is, God's church. He reminded them "that God's Spirit lives" within them. Since this is true, Paul continued, *"If anyone destroys God's temple, God will destroy him; for God's temple is sacred, and you are that temple"* (1 Cor. 3:16).

What was Paul saying? There can be no other meaning. He warned that any Christian leader who deliberately destroys, divides, and dismantles God's unique workmanship—His body of believers—is in danger of being destroyed by God Himself. This is what happened to the sons of Eli. God is warning us through Paul that it can happen to any spiritual leader who takes advantage of God's people. The Lord is particularly grieved when we destroy love and unity, the very things Jesus prayed for as He went toward the cross to die for the sins of the world in order to give birth to His most prized possession—the church of Jesus Christ.

Principle 3. It's possible for children to grow up to be godly men and women, even though they have lived in an environment that is permeated with evil.

This is one of the most encouraging principles that grows out of this unique story. In spite of his evil environment, Samuel continued to mature and become a man of God. If this could happen to this young man in his environment, it certainly can happen to our own children.

However, this does not happen automatically. We must "play by God's rules." Most importantly, we must live consistent Christian lives in front of our children from the very time they are born. We must dedicate them to the Lord early and pray for them consistently. We must also do all we can to protect them from evil influences without attempting to remove them completely from the world.

This, of course, is one of the greatest challenges we face as parents in the world today. But, when we join together as Christian parents and encourage and pray for one another, I'm confident God will help us to bring up our children "in the training and instruction of the Lord" (Eph. 6:4). If it was possible in the first-century world, it's certainly possible in our deteriorating twentieth-century world.

Personalizing These Principles

The following questions and comments are designed to help you apply these principles in your life today.

1. Are you justifying sin in your life simply because everything seems to be going well at the moment? If so, remember that God is long-suffering and gracious, but eventually He'll discipline His children who deliberately and persistently live outside of His will. It will happen!

2. As a Christian leader, are you taking deliberate advantage of God's people through some form of dishonesty or manipulation, or are you simply living an inconsistent life? If so, remember the words of James: "Not many of you should presume to be teachers, my brothers, because

you know that we who teach will be judged more strictly" (James 3:1).

3. Are you doing all you can to be a consistent parent who is modeling Christianity to his children?

Set a Goal

Ask the Holy Spirit to reveal to you which principle needs the most attention in your life? Then, set a personal goal:

_____

_____

_____

_____

Memorize the Following Scripture

So whether you eat or drink or whatever you do, do it all for the glory of God. Do not cause anyone to stumble, whether Jews, Greeks or the church of God
1 CORINTHIANS 10:31–32

Growing Together

The following questions are designed for small group discussion:

1. Without being judgmental and critical, can you think of examples in which Christians have suffered serious consequences because they have chosen to allow sin to control their lives? Has this ever happened in your extended family? What resulted? Most importantly, what lessons can we all learn from these examples?

2. Why does God hold Christian leaders more responsible for their sinful actions? Why did Paul write to Titus and say that sinful leaders "must be silenced"? (Titus 1:11).

3. What can we do, particularly as Christian parents, to help our children grow up to live productive Christian lives? What have you found to be effective with your own children? Is it possible to be too strict? What are some of the pitfalls we must avoid that might cause us to be counterproductive in our child-rearing approaches?

4. In what way can we pray for you specifically?

Chapter 6

The Voice in the Night
Read 1 Samuel 3:1–21

*O*ne of the most difficult things we face as men is to admit mistakes, especially those that have negatively impacted our families. It's tough to say, "I've failed!" All of us can identify with that struggle. But down deep, we also know that honesty is the only way to handle our failures. Everyone admires a man who faces reality.

Eli was a great man, but he failed to "restrain his sons" and to correct them. He even participated in some of their wrong-doing. But what made Eli an even greater man is that he accepted full responsibility for his actions. We see no excuses, no rationalizations, no sidestepping, no placing the blame on others. Though he "reaped what he had sown," he did not depart this life shaking his fist at God!

Samuel's Protector

While Eli's sons continued their evil practices and descent into a mire of sin, "the boy Samuel continued to grow in stature and in favor with the LORD and with men" (1 Sam. 2:26). This is truly amazing—and encouraging! We have a clue as to how this happened when we read that "the boy Samuel ministered before the LORD *under Eli*" (3:1, emphasis mine; see also 2:11). Though this young impressionable lad rubbed shoulders with Eli's evil sons,

Hophni and Phinehas, this old priest must have "built a hedge" around Samuel, becoming his protector.

Eli knew all about his sons' sinful behavior (3:23). He also knew that he had not dealt with this situation properly, even participating in their sin by eating "the choice parts" of the meat offered by the children of Israel (2:29).

Eli also knew he and his sons would suffer the consequences. This is why I believe he faced the situation head-on, warning Samuel not to be influenced by their sin. Though God is certainly able to protect innocent children from bad adult influences, He normally uses people to do it—particularly parents.Consequently, Eli must have taken Samuel under his "wing" and carefully nurtured him in the Word of God without actually removing him from the evil environment in Shiloh.

What Eli had failed to do for his own sons, he could now do for Samuel. Though Hophni and Phinehas would not listen to his warnings (2:25), Samuel did. He opened his heart to his elderly friend and mentor and must have determined not to follow in the footsteps of Eli's wicked sons.

When God Stopped Speaking

We're not told Samuel's age on that awesome night when God spoke directly to this young lad. However, several years must have gone by after "a man of God" pronounced judgment on Eli's household (2:27). In fact, after this revelation from heaven, God had stopped speaking directly to His people on a regular basis. We read that "in those days the word of the LORD was rare; there were not many visions" (3:1b).

Samuel was probably a young teenager at this point in his life, since the Hebrew word used to describe Samuel in this passage is *naar*, which was used to describe a person from infancy to adolescence. Perhaps he was approximately the same age as Mary when the angel Gabriel announced that she would become the mother of God's special Son, Jesus Christ (Luke 1:26–38).

Here I Am

We're given another clue that a substantial period of time had passed. Eli had aged. His eyesight had deteriorated to the point he "could barely see" (1 Sam. 3:2).

The old priest lay sleeping in his usual place. Samuel, too, had retired, probably to one of the small rooms that was built in the outer court for the priests and the Levites to live in while they were serving in the tabernacle. It was still dark when God spoke to Samuel (3:3).[1]

Understandably, Samuel thought the voice he heard was Eli's. Knowing the high priest's physical condition, he may have thought Eli was calling for help. He ran quickly to Eli's side, saying, "Here I am; you called me!" (3:5).

Thinking Samuel was probably dreaming, Eli assured Samuel he had not called for him. However, when this happened three times in succession, Eli suddenly realized that God was attempting to get Samuel's attention (3:6–8).

Speak, Lord

What an incredible experience this must have been for young Samuel! One of the most unique experiences in life is to receive a direct revelation from God. We know from other scriptural accounts that it is an awesome experience—one never to be taken lightly. For the apostle Paul it was so overpowering, he was struck blind when Jesus Christ called his name from heaven (Acts 9:3–9). Later, when he was miraculously "caught up to the third heaven" and "heard inexpressible things," God allowed Paul to experience an ongoing "thorn" in his flesh to keep him from "becoming conceited because of these surpassingly great revelations" (2 Cor. 12:1–10). And when the apostle John saw Jesus Christ on the island of Patmos, he "fell at his feet as though dead" (Rev. 1:17).

A New Experience

Samuel had never heard God's voice. Though he was destined to become a great prophet, up to this point in time "the word of the LORD had not yet been revealed to him" (1 Sam. 3:7).

Since this was a new experience for Samuel, he had no way of understanding and interpreting what was happening. But Eli did. When Samuel heard a voice the third time, Eli told his young friend to go back and lie down and, if he heard the voice again, to say, "Speak, LORD, for your servant is listening" (3:9).

As we might imagine, when God spoke yet a fourth time, He had Samuel's undivided attention. But the Lord's message was very troubling and threatening (3:11–14). God reiterated the judgment He was going to bring on Eli's household. The Lord made one point very clear to Samuel: since Hophni and Phinehas had "made themselves contemptible," God was going to bring judgment on Eli's whole household because "he failed to restrain them" (3:13).

An Awesome Message

Was Samuel totally surprised at this message from God? Perhaps not as much as we might think. If Eli had discussed his sons' sins with his young attendant—which I believe he had—then Samuel already knew Eli's concerns. Eli may have shared with Samuel that God had spoken once before and had given this same basic message through another "man of God."

Whatever Samuel knew ahead of time, he now understood more fully the seriousness of Eli's failure as a father and the penalty his household would face. God's final statement to Samuel was particularly sobering: "the guilt of Eli's house will never be atoned for by sacrifice or offering" (3:14)!

Samuel's Fear

Samuel was afraid to tell Eli what God had said. Though he "lay down until morning," his eyes were probably wide open (3:15). When he rose to carry out his daily duties, the first of which was to open the doors of the Tabernacle, his thoughts must have been racing and his heart pounding. How could he discuss this foreboding message with this elderly man who had become his spiritual father?

In spite of his weaknesses, however, Eli was an old sage! He anticipated bad news and was ready to face reality. In fact, when he asked Samuel to tell him what God had said, he warned his young friend to be totally open and honest (3:17)—as if to teach Samuel a very important lesson that he had learned the hard way. Samuel must be a faithful prophet. He must never withhold or soften God's message to sinful humanity—even if it hurt those closest to him. Eli had failed to do that very thing with his own sons and he didn't want Samuel to repeat his mistakes.

A Bittersweet Experience

What Samuel relayed to Eli only confirmed what he already knew. "He is the Lord," Eli responded, "let him do what is good in his eyes" (3:18).

Eli took God's words of judgment like a man. He knew he had failed, and he was not going to try to rationalize away what had happened. He took full responsibility for his actions. He was well aware he was dealing with a holy and sovereign God. Furthermore, he understood as never before that Samuel would be his successor. Though God's message was terribly painful, Eli must have been somewhat comforted when he realized that he had been given the privilege of preparing this young man for the great task that lay ahead of him. This was one of the most bittersweet experiences he had ever faced.

Letting Go

Though details are sketchy, it's clear that Eli began to "let go" of his position as judge in Israel. He knew that God had raised up Samuel to be a prophet and leader—to do some things he had not accomplished.

As Samuel grew older, God continued to speak to and through him. Whatever God said He was going to do, He brought to pass. Not one word fell "to the ground" unfulfilled (3:19). Furthermore, we read: "And all Israel from Dan to Beersheba recognized that Samuel was attested as a prophet of the LORD. The LORD continued to appear at Shiloh, and there he revealed himself to Samuel through his word. And Samuel's word came to all Israel" (3:20–4:1a).

Becoming God's Man Today

Principles to Live By

What can we learn from these dramatic experiences that will help us face life as mature Christian men? Several biblical guidelines stand out boldly:

Principle 1. Though we "reap what we sow," even in the midst of utter failure, God has unique ways to give us a second chance.

He did this for Eli. What Eli couldn't redo for his sons, he was able to achieve in Samuel's life. Though it must have been very painful to use his own sons as negative examples, nevertheless, he must have often warned Samuel to never follow in their footsteps.

And so it is in our lives today. As fathers, we may have failed our own children. The damage may seem irreparable. But we must never give up on our children, particularly in terms of praying for them. Remember that "under law" no divine and perfect mediator existed to intercede before the Father. When earthly sacrifices and offerings were rejected by the Lord, even the high priest in Israel could not intercede (2:25). But "under grace," and in light of the "new covenant," the great High Priest, Jesus Christ, is interceding for us moment by moment (Heb. 7:26; 8:1–2). He has provided a "new and living way" into the presence of God (10:20). The only thing that ultimately separates anyone from God is a hardened heart and final unbelief. There is always hope while our children are on this side of eternity.

What can we do while we pray and wait? Here we can learn a great lesson from Eli. You, too, can find a "Samuel," a "Timothy"—a young man who has no father who will respond to a loving and sensitive father image. Because of the multitude of broken homes in our culture, there are thousands of young men who each need a mentor—someone who can demonstrate the realities of Christianity. God is giving fathers an opportunity to do with other boys what they may have failed to do with their own sons.

Principle 2. We must never allow ourselves to blame God or anyone else for our failures.

Eli illustrates this principle as no other Old Testament man of character. Though he failed miserably as a father, he never blamed his wife, his sons, the circumstances, the children of Israel, or God for what happened. How easy it would have been to become bitter. But there is no evidence he ever did. He never made anyone else the villain and himself a victim.

A Painful Experience

As a pastor I've had to confront people who are living in sin. I'm thinking of a man and a woman who had violated their respective marriage vows and had committed adultery. Eventually they were discovered, and they admitted their sin and sought forgiveness from their spouses and the church.

Thinking they had truly repented, we did all we could to support them. We laid out a plan for recovery and restoration involving accountability groups for all parties involved—including the wounded marital partners.

Personally, I was very encouraged and hopeful. I really believed we were going to see healing and ultimate restoration. It was a definite possibility. I loved these people dearly, and I was willing to do anything I could to help them recover from the devastating results of their sins. But sadly, we discovered what appeared to be sincere sorrow for their sins turned out to be more emotional than real. They continued communicating with each other and had to once again be confronted. At this point, they both moved into the "victim role." They started blaming others for the problem they themselves created.

A Victim Mentality

This is a natural tendency for people who are trapped because of their sins and who don't admit it totally and take full responsibility for their actions. They put the blame for their failure on other people. This is what we call a "victim mentality." Eli could have easily fallen into this trap—but he didn't. He made no excuses and accepted full responsibility for his failure as a father.

Fortunately, most of us don't face the judgment Eli faced. There's hope and forgiveness in Jesus Christ, no matter our failures. Though our families may be affected for years to come, there is no need to allow the results of the sin to move into the next generation. True repentance and seeking forgiveness can bring incredible healing in most situations—including moral failure.

Principle 3. We must never fail to accept the fact that it's time to "let go," to "step aside," and to allow someone else to do what we cannot do.

Eli's experience is unique, of course. Hopefully, none of us will ever have to step aside as he did because of God's judgment on our lives. But there is a broader principle that grows out of his reaction to the prophetic messages from both the unnamed "man of God" and the young man who would grow up to replace him. He accepted reality with grace and dignity.

We All Need Each Other

This principle applies in many situations. We all face circumstances where we need help in solving problems—in rearing our families, in dealing with wayward children, in carrying out our vocational responsibilities. Unfortunately, it's easy for pride and ego to get in the way—to stop us from seeking help. When we do, we ignore the great truth that we are but one member of the "body of Christ" and God has designed the "body"—that is, the church—so that we are dependent on other "members of the body" to enable us to succeed as Christians. Nothing could be more clear in the New Testament (1 Cor. 12:21–27; Eph. 4:11–16).

Beware of the "Old-Age Syndrome"

This principle is particularly relevant to those of us who are growing older. More specifically, it applies to those of us in the ministry. I've seen successful pastors who have come to the place where "they need the church" more than "the church needs them." This also happens to businessmen, particularly to those who own their own companies and have the authority to determine their destinies.

Though we all need to feel successful at what we're doing, when our emotional needs begin to drive us and blur our thinking, we've stepped over the line. We hang on too long! And when we do, "self" rather than "Christ" has become the center of our lives. Every older man—including yours truly—needs to be aware of this basic tendency and the damage we can do to the very people we love the most!

Principle 4. God wants to speak clearly and regularly to all of us through the Holy Scriptures.

Though Samuel's experience was unique, God wants all of us to approach His Word by saying, "Speak, LORD, for your servant is listening" (1 Sam. 3:9).

Think for a moment what we know about God's will that Samuel never knew. Today we can even know more about God's eternal plan for our lives than most of the apostles of Jesus Christ. The reason is pure and simple. We have God's final and complete revelation as it is contained both in the Old and New Testaments. And every time we approach the Word of God and read it or hear it taught, we should ask the Holy Spirit to speak to us and to help us apply God's eternal truth to our lives. With the Psalmist of old, we need to pray, "Open my eyes that I may see wonderful things in your law" (Ps. 119:18). When we do, God will speak directly to our hearts.

Personalizing These Principles

The following questions will help you make these principles a part of your own life. Think about them carefully and respond honestly.

1. If you feel that you have failed God as a father—or in some other role—are you looking for opportunities to do for others what you may not have been able to do for your own children?

   At this point you may have guilt and a sense of condemnation that God wants to remove from your heart. Remember the words of John: "If we confess our sins, he is faithful and just and will forgive us our sins and purify us from all unrighteousness" (1 John 1:9).

2. Are you blaming others for your own mistakes and sins?

You may need to think about this question carefully and prayerfully since it's easy for all of us to rationalize and deceive ourselves. As you reflect on this question, read David's prayer in Psalm 51.

3. Are you allowing pride and self-centered needs and interests to keep you from allowing someone else to do what you can no longer do effectively?

As you reflect on this question, meditate on Paul's words to the Corinthians in 1 Corinthians 12:21–27.

4. Do you read the Word of God regularly, asking the Holy Spirit to speak to you through the Scriptures?

As you reflect on this question, meditate on the following verse of Scripture: "For the word of God is living and active. Sharper than any double-edged sword, it penetrates even to dividing soul and spirit, joints and marrow; it judges the thoughts and attitudes of the heart" (Heb. 4:12).

Set a Goal

As a result of the process you've just gone through, what one goal do you need to set for your life? Ask the Holy Spirit to reveal the area in your life you need to adjust and bring into conformity with His will.

_____

_____

_____

_____

Memorize the Following Scripture

For the word of God is living and active. Sharper than any double-edged sword, it penetrates even to dividing soul and spirit, joints and marrow; it judges the thoughts and attitudes of the heart.
HEBREWS 4:12

Growing Together

The following questions are designed for small group discussion:

1. In what ways has God given you opportunities to correct mistakes you've made in the past?

2. If you've ever allowed yourself to develop a "victim mentality," would you feel free to share the experience with us? How were you able to change your perceptions?

3. Would you be willing to share some experiences where you have been unwilling to "let go" and to allow others to do what you could not as effectively? How did you overcome this problem?

4. Why is it so important to meditate on the Scriptures regularly, asking the Holy Spirit to enlighten our hearts and minds? How have you found this to be a significant life-changing experience?

5. In what way can we pray for you personally?

Chapter 7

A Serious Error in Judgment
Read 1 Samuel 4:1–22

*A*ll of us can make errors in judgment, regardless of our age, experience, wisdom, or personal relationship with God. It is true we're more vulnerable when we're young and inexperienced, but this malady is no respecter of age.

We're about to see this reality fleshed out in some dramatic ways. We'll also see the tragic consequences. But as always, we'll learn some valuable principles that will help us avoid making the same mistakes.

Gaining Perspective

At this moment in Israel's history, God had delivered His people "into the hands of the Philistines." As so often is recorded in the Book of Judges, "the Israelites did evil in the eyes of the LORD" and brought judgment on themselves. This period of domination and control lasted "for forty years" (Judg. 13:1). At some point during this period of time, Samuel was born and was destined to help lead Israel back into God's will and out of this bondage.

We've already observed the miraculous events surrounding Samuel's birth. We've also noted how he grew "in stature and in favor with the LORD and with men" (1 Sam. 2:26), even though he was surrounded by the evil antics and immoral behavior of Eli's sons, Hophni and Phinehas (2:12–17, 22). And in the previous chapter, we saw how God revealed Himself to this young man. Samuel heard God's "voice in the night" at a time when "the word of the LORD was rare" (3:1). Through these unique events, we once again see God's amazing grace being extended to His people—in spite of their personal and national sins.

Samuel's initial nocturnal experience with the Lord was just the beginning of a series of direct revelations. In turn, Samuel faithfully communicated God's message to the people of Israel. Again and again every detail in Samuel's prophecies came true. The Lord "let none of his words fall to the ground" (3:19). Everyone recognized that Samuel was indeed a true prophet (3:20). He had passed the test outlined by the Lord when Moses reviewed the Law for all Israel prior to their entrance into the Promised Land. Listen to Moses' words: "You may say to yourselves, 'How can we know when a message has not been spoken by the LORD?' If what a prophet proclaims in the name of the LORD does not take place or come true, that is a message the LORD has not spoken. That prophet has spoken presumptuously. Do not be afraid of him" (Deut. 18:21–22).

A Word from God or Man?

One day something happened that no one anticipated. Samuel told the Israelites to go out and "fight against the Philistines" (4:1). Though the English translation is a bit nebulous as to the exact details, it's clear this order came from Samuel and was delivered "to all Israel" (4:1a).

Did this "word" originate with God or Samuel? It's obvious the leaders in Israel definitely believed that God had spoken. After all, the Lord had "continued to appear" to Samuel, and every time this young man passed God's message on to the children of Israel, every aspect of that message came true. Why shouldn't they take seriously Samuel's word to go out to do battle against their archenemies?

Bad Advice

Unfortunately, what Samuel passed on to the leaders in Israel was "his word"—not God's direct revelation. This is why we read very specifically—"and *Samuel's word* came to all Israel" (4:1a). In the Hebrew text, it's clear that this is in contrast to the "word of the LORD." We must remember that "all words" prophets spoke were not from God. Like all of us, they made judgments on their own and communicated those judgments to others—just as we do today. At other times they had direct messages from God that they passed on to others. This clearly seems to be an example where Samuel was communicating his own thoughts and ideas to Israel.[1]

Don't misunderstand. Samuel was not deliberately deceiving Israel by passing on a message he claimed he had received from God but hadn't. Rather, he may have been carried away with his own sense of "calling" that he was to be Israel's deliverer. After all, he had had some awesome experiences: God had spoken to him directly when there were very few divine revelations, and he continued to receive these messages. It's very conceivable that Samuel, at this moment in his life, stepped out ahead of the Lord and made a bad judgment.

Men of God Are Still Men

If Samuel made a serious error in judgment, it's not surprising. It happened to Moses—one of the greatest Old Testament prophets who ever lived (Deut. 34:10–12). Yet, he stepped out ahead of the Lord and tried to deliver Israel in his own strength. Since he had been "educated in all the wisdom of the Egyptians and was powerful in speech and action" (Acts 7:22), he found it easy to believe that the children of Israel would conclude "that God was using him to rescue them" from Egyptian bondage (7:25). Wrong! They rejected his efforts!

Unfortunately, Moses was not responding to a "vision from God" when he came to the defense of his fellow Israelites and killed an Egyptian. Rather, in his humanness, he had "visions of grandeur" relative to his own abilities and calling—which led to terrible failure and forty years on the backside of the desert.

Though Samuel was also destined to become a great prophet of God, remember that he was no more perfect than Moses—and much, much younger. Could it be that in his youthful passion and spirit, and in the context of his uninterrupted success as a faithful prophet, he stepped out ahead of the Lord and set Israel up for failure? Could it be that what was about to happen to Israel was Samuel's first major lesson in humility? If so—and I believe it was—it would be a lesson he would never forget!

Tragedy on the Battlefield

Israel's leaders responded to Samuel's advice. With great boldness and confidence in the message they had just received from their young spiritual leader and judge, the men of Israel "went out to fight against the Philistines" (1 Sam. 4:1b). Hearing they were coming, the Philistines mobilized with a counterattack and wiped out four thousand of Israel's fighting men. The rest of the army had to retreat. They were utterly "defeated by the Philistines" (4:2)—and disillusioned. How could this have happened?

A Foolish Question

What happened that day left the elders and leaders in Israel totally bewildered and perplexed. Calling an emergency meeting to assess the situation, they focused on one basic question—"Why did the LORD bring defeat upon us today before the Philistines?" (4:3a).

This question makes it clear that these leaders in Israel believed that Samuel's message to attack the Philistines was from God. Consequently, they didn't understand this defeat. Why would the Lord set them up for failure?

Though this seemed like a logical question to these men, in essence it was very foolish. If they had stopped to evaluate their own sinful lifestyles, the immorality that existed in their own priesthood, and their own violation of God's instructions regarding worship and sacrifice, they would have taken an "inward look" rather than putting the blame on God. They would have also consulted with Samuel to see if they had "missed something." If they had such confidence in his status as a prophet, why did they seemingly ignore him? Is it possible that down deep they actually knew the answer to their own foolish question—but chose to ignore reality?

A Foolish Decision

Whatever their thoughts and motives, Israel's leaders took matters into their own hands. Rather than assessing the situation objectively and prayerfully, attempting to discern the real reasons why they experienced defeat at the hands of the Philistines, the elders of Israel panicked. Their "foolish question" led them to make a very prideful and "foolish decision." They tried to manipulate God—to use the ark of the covenant as a spiritual "rabbit's foot." Thus we read: "'Let us bring the ark of the LORD's covenant from Shiloh, so that it may go with us and save us from the hand of our enemies'" (4:3).

Israel's Selective Memory

The elders of Israel correctly knew that God had chosen to reveal His presence in a special way over the ark of the covenant where He would dwell between the cherubim (Exod. 25:22; 1 Sam. 4:4). They had also heard of Israel's miraculous victories in the past associated with the ark. Perhaps they had recalled during this moment of panic that unforgettable story of the walls of Jericho. Under Joshua's leadership, the army of God had marched around this fortified city, carrying the ark of the covenant (Josh. 6:6,11,13). And without "shooting an arrow" or "throwing a spear" the walls collapsed when the priests blew their trumpets and "all the people gave a loud shout" (6:20).

But the elders of Israel in Samuel's day either forgot or ignored a very important reason for the miraculous victory at Jericho and in subsequent battles. Israel was successful when they obeyed God's laws (Josh. 1:6–7).

Sadly, the children of Israel in Samuel's day ignored these spiritual conditions. They marched off to face the Philistines with "Eli's two sons, Hophni and Phinehas," accompanying "the ark of the covenant of God" (1 Sam. 4:4b). Here were two "spiritual leaders" who epitomized disobedience to God's moral and sacrificial laws and had already led many in Israel to commit the same sins. What a foolish decision on the part of the elders of Israel!

The Plan Backfires

When Hophni and Phinehas arrived in Israel's encampment with the ark of the covenant, every man armed for battle shouted so loudly that the ground shook (4:5). In fact, when the Philistines heard what was happening they were scared to death (4:6). They too had heard about the "ark of the LORD." They had even heard about what had happened to the Egyptian army when they attempted to stop Moses from leading the children of Israel across the Red Sea. Though they had certain facts confused regarding Israel's history and interpreted what they knew of Israel's victories from a pagan perspective, they were convinced they were in serious trouble. "Who will deliver us from the hand of these mighty gods?" they cried (4:8).

Predictably, Israel's plan backfired. Their battle strategy only served to ignite the emotions of their enemies. The

Philistines became more determined to defeat Israel (4:9). When they heard their own commander shout, "Be men, and fight," they did just that. With massive doses of adrenaline flowing into each man's bloodstream, they once again went up to meet Israel on the battlefield.

A Horrendous Catastrophe

Israel's initial battle with the Philistines was minor compared with this second confrontation. Thirty thousand men lost their lives, compared with the previous four thousand (4:10). Those who managed to escape death fled. And during this battle God allowed to happen what He had revealed to Eli through an "unnamed man of God" (2:34) and had confirmed to young Samuel (3:11–14). Both "Hophni and Phinehas died" on the same day (4:11).

Thinking the "ark of God" was magical and uniquely divine in itself, the Philistines captured this beautiful gold-laden box made of acacia wood (Exod. 25:10–11). In doing so, the Philistines only proved that God had not accompanied the Israelites into battle as they thought He would. If God had enthroned Himself over the ark, every Philistine who touched it would have dropped dead! In fact, Hophni and Phinehas would have probably been struck dead long before they died at the hands of the Philistines. You see, God had not been uniquely present in the Holy of Holies in the tabernacle for a long time. Though He had begun to reveal divine messages through Samuel, He was not "with Israel" as He had been during the days of Moses and Joshua.[2]

A Dismal Report

The very same day the army of Israel suffered its second tragic defeat, a messenger ran back to Shiloh and reported what had happened (4:12). Predictably, the word spread rapidly throughout the city, creating a state of panic (4:13). Imagine the fear that must have gripped the hearts of wives and mothers when they heard the extent of the slaughter. Out of thirty thousand deaths, the probability that their husbands had died must have created incredible paranoia.

The wailing and crying throughout the city quickly reached the ears of old Eli who was "sitting on his chair by the side of the road" (4:13). Ever since his sons had left that city with the ark of God, he had been paralyzed with fear.

Eli's Tragic Death

Facing reality—as Eli was prone to do—but fearing the worst, he asked what had happened (4:14, 16). He no doubt anticipated the bad news regarding his sons. Clearly his greatest concern focused on the ark. When he heard that the Philistines had captured it, he fell off his chair backward and broke his neck, probably dying within minutes (4:17–18).

How tragic! After ruling Israel for a total of forty years, this old priest met his Maker in the midst of a horrible situation. What grieved him the most in those parting moments on earth was that Israel—and particularly his sons—had so deliberately departed from doing the will of God. He must have felt like a total failure—as a father and as high priest in Israel (2:27–36; 3:11–14). What a terrible way to die! The physical pain he experienced from a "broken neck" must have paled in the midst of the emotional pain he felt because of his "broken soul."

Ichabod

The results of Israel's defeat impacted many young lives and mothers but none so sadly as Eli's "daughter-in-law, the wife of Phinehas" (4:19). She was pregnant and her loss was even more tragic than Eli's. She not only lost a good friend when her father-in-law died, but she also lost her husband. She too must have been very concerned about Phinehas' spiritual condition.

No one knew the sins of her husband like this woman. Her heart must have been gripped with fear along with Eli's when she saw Phinehas leave Shiloh, walking beside the ark of God. Though she had put up with his infidelity and idolatry all her married life, she knew that judgment must soon be coming and that eventually God's hand would fall on her evil husband.

When it happened, however, it was more than she could bear. She went into early labor and died shortly after her son was born. When she discovered she had given birth to a little boy, she simply looked the other way, whispered his name and took her last breath. We read: "She named the boy Ichabod, saying, 'The glory has departed from Israel'—because of the capture of the ark of God and the deaths of her father-in-law and her husband. She said, 'The glory has departed from Israel, for the ark of God has been captured'" (4:21–22).

This mother's final words give us an even deeper glimpse into her heart. She represents those women of faith who have lived with men who have been anything but spiritual. What grieved her the most was not his death—for that would have ultimately been a blessing. She was more deeply concerned about what had happened to the ark of God.

Becoming God's Man Today

Principles to Live By

This is an awesome passage of Scripture. The specific events described are difficult for most of us to identify with, but as always there are some powerful principles that emerge from this Old Testament story.

Principle 1. We must always evaluate the advice we receive in light of God's revealed truth in the Holy Scriptures, even when that advice is given by a godly leader.

There's no question that Samuel was devoted to doing the will of God. But he was also a very young man who had been given an awesome responsibility directly from God Himself. If the great apostle Paul was prone to become prideful when he was "caught up to the third heaven" and received "surpassingly great revelations" (2 Cor. 12:2, 7), think of young Samuel who had heard God's voice many times.

No Respecter of Age

If Samuel had been more mature, he would have called for national repentance rather than sending the armies of Israel to do battle against the Philistines. He instead made a serious and costly error in judgment—one I'm confident he would never forget.

It's true that young men are more prone to judgment errors, simply because they lack experience. But this kind of mistake is no respecter of age. We must remember that as we grow older, we normally face more complex problems which call for more complex resolutions. Consequently, older men can make some serious errors in judgment as well. And remember that it was the elders (the older leaders) in Israel who decided to transport the ark of God onto the battlefield. This was a horrible error in judgment—much more arrogant and devastating than Samuel's initial mistake.

Consulting the Scriptures

Let's not lose sight of the principle. It's important to always evaluate advice in the light of God's complete revelation as we have it in the Scriptures. In this sense, we have a great advantage over the children of Israel. We can look to God's written Word directly.

This does not mean that we should not consult with others, since this is also a biblical principle. What we've learned from this story, however, is that no matter what we're told, we need to evaluate that advice with God's written revelation in the Bible. As we do, we should also consult other mature Christians to make sure we're interpreting God's Word correctly.

Principle 2. When we violate God's directives and suffer the consequences, this is the moment to confess our sins and refocus our thoughts on God's will for our lives—not to try to dig ourselves out of the mess we've created by taking another step out of His will.

When we face a crisis, and particularly failure, we need to search our hearts. This does not necessarily mean we're out of God's will because we're experiencing negative results, but it is certainly the time to "take a look" at our attitudes and actions. And if we already know or discover in the process that we are disobeying God's Word, we need to pray with David of old: "Create in me a pure heart, O God, and renew a steadfast spirit within me" (Ps. 51:10).

Principle 3. A life of sin not only affects our own relationship with God and our eternal destiny, but it impacts and hurts others who are close to us.

Think of what happened because of Samuel's initial error in judgment. Fortunately, most of us do not face this kind of tragic result when we make errors in judgment. But when we fail God, others are always hurt to one degree or another. This reality should motivate us to do God's will more faithfully. Loved ones often suffer because of circumstances beyond our control. God forbid that we cause others to suffer because of circumstances that are within our control.

The impact is even more devastating when people suffer because of serious sins in our lives. Think of the people who have been hurt by the failure of spiritual leaders. I can think of one well-known pastor whose family has been devastated because of his immorality. His children have actually turned against God! Furthermore, many Christians who consulted this man for guidance are wandering in the wilderness, still disillusioned. They have not fallen mortally wounded in battle, but they are experiencing deep wounds in their souls that may never be healed apart from a miracle of God's grace.

The same can be said of husbands who have divorced their wives to marry other women, fathers who have forsaken their families, and men who have turned their backs on God. What pain this has caused—in the immediate family as well as the extended family. Nothing is so devastating as a home that breaks up because of selfishness, insensitivity, misunderstandings, immorality, and other serious sins.

Thank God this need not happen! With God's help we can walk through this world, keeping "in step with the Spirit" (Gal. 5:25), reflecting His fruit: "love, joy, peace, patience, kindness, goodness, faithfulness, gentleness and self-control" (5:22–23).

Principle 4. Though there are times God seemingly gives up on sinful humanity, it is never too late to cry out to the Lord for help and restoration.

Paul stated in his letter to the Romans—three times in fact—that there are times God gives men and women over to follow their own sinful desires (Rom. 1:24, 26, 28). However, this does not mean that these people are doomed to die in their sins. If Hophni and Phinehas had turned to God, He would have forgiven them. And so it is with all of us. It is never too late to turn back to God, to confess our sins, and to experience total forgiveness.

This does not mean that we can undo everything in the past. We may have to live with the results of our sins and mistakes. Samuel certainly couldn't raise thirty-four thousand men from the dead. But he could go forward and learn from this serious error in judgment and become an even better spiritual leader in Israel. What about you?

Personalizing These Principles

Use the following questions and comments to help you apply these biblical principles.

1. To what extent do I evaluate advice and counsel—even from people I consider godly—in light of the teachings and Scripture?

   A word of caution: Don't take this principle so seriously it makes you skeptical and insecure. Furthermore, don't feel you need to do a scriptural evaluation on your own. Consult other godly friends and spiritual leaders.

2. Is pride keeping me from admitting my failures and mistakes? If so, the answer is to humble myself before God and others and seek forgiveness.

   No matter how hard we attempt to apply biblical principles in solving life's problems, we'll always make mistakes. Our goal should always be to keep these mistakes minimal. To achieve this goal, we must always consult God's Word first and simultaneously consult other godly Christians. The key is to be teachable.

   On the other hand, if we've made mistakes because we're purposely ignoring God's will for our life, we need to go back to "square one," start over again, and "keep in step with God's Spirit," attempting to correct our inappropriate decisions (James 3:13–16).

3. When you make a decision, do you stop and think how this might impact others—your marital partner, your children, your Christian friends, your other brothers and sisters in Christ, and those who do not know Christ (1 Cor. 10:31–11:1)?

4. If you have failed God and feel hopeless, to what extent have you turned back to God, asking for forgiveness? It

is never too late to turn back. No matter what our failures, God will forgive (1 John 1:9).

Set a Goal

As a result of this personal evaluation, what one goal would you like to set for your life? Ask the Holy Spirit to unveil a special need.

_____

_____

_____

_____

Memorize the Following Scripture

If any of you lacks wisdom, he should ask God, who gives generously to all without finding fault, and it will be given to him.
JAMES 1:5

Growing Together

The following questions are designed for small group discussion:

1. What is your personal strategy for making wise decisions?

2. What experience can you share to encourage all of us to avoid attempting to solve our problems by taking another step out of God's will?

3. How have your mistakes and judgment errors impacted those closest to you? How have you attempted to correct the situation? What were the results?

4. What advice do you have for those who may feel God has given up on them?

5. In what way can we pray for you personally?

Chapter 8

Doing Things God's Way

Read 1 Samuel 7:1–17

*T*he week I was putting the finishing touches on this chapter, I received a call from a businessman I had been meeting with on Thursday mornings to work through my book *The Measure of a Man*.[1] Jim has been through his own very difficult journey. By his own confession, for a couple of years he did things more "his way" than "God's way." But Jim is back where he belongs—committed to doing God's will and not his own. In fact, he has been meeting with another Christian businessman who has also wandered in his own barren wilderness.

When Jim called, I could hear excitement in his voice. "Gene," he said, "my friend just told me that I'm right! There's only one way to be truly fulfilled in life and that's to do things God's way."

Though a prophet of God, Samuel had to learn this lesson the hard way—and so did the rest of the children of Israel. In this study we'll see a wonderful 180-degree turn in the lives of God's people—but only after a twenty-year period of trying to straddle the proverbial fence when it came to doing things God's way.

A Dramatic Backdrop

The army of Israel faced an incredible disaster when they followed young Samuel's advice to make war with the Philistines. Not only were they soundly defeated, suffering multiple thousands of casualties, but the Philistine army captured the ark of God and carried it to Ashdod, their capital city, and placed it in their own temple beside their god Dagon (5:1–2).

Though God had removed His special presence from the ark, He still demonstrated to the Philistines that this gold-covered box had powerful spiritual influence. When the people of Ashdod entered the temple the next morning, their stone god had toppled face first to the ground in front of the ark (5:3). Thinking it was an accident, the Ashdodites set their god back in place. But the following morning, the same thing had happened—but this time, Dagon's head and hands were lying in a separate heap (5:4).

God's Hand of Judgment

To demonstrate further that this was no mere fluke, the Lord followed this event by afflicting the people of Ashdod with rectal tumors—a very discomforting disease to say the least. To add to their misery, the Lord also devastated their crops. We read that "the Lord's hand was heavy upon the people of Ashdod and its vicinity" (5:6).

The men of Ashdod certainly wasted no time seeking a solution to this horrendous problem. They recognized that "the god of Israel" had caused this calamity (5:7). Though they describe the Lord as just another "god," they acknowledged that this "god" had more power than Dagon.

A Naive Solution

The Philistines' solution reveals their limited perspective on who they were dealing with. They believed that moving the ark to another city would solve the problem. Ironically, they did not ultimately remove the problem but simply moved it to the city of Gath (5:8), where the same thing happened all over again. When the ark of God arrived, so did the tumors. We read that "The Lord's hand was against that city, throwing it into a great panic" (5:9).

By this time, the Philistines should have realized that they were dealing with a problem that couldn't be resolved by simply moving the ark from one location to another. However, they tried again, moving the ark to Ekron (5:10). But the Lord intensified the devastation. We read that "God's hand was very heavy upon it" (5:11). People were not only plagued with tumors but people were dying throughout the city.

A Wise Decision

After seven months, the Lord finally got the Philistines' undivided attention (6:1). Simply moving the ark from city to city not only left the problem unresolved but intensified the disease and devastation. The Philistine leaders finally decided they needed to remove the ark of God completely—to send it back to Israel. Realizing, however, this was a problem with supernatural ramifications, they arranged a meeting with their own priests and diviners. "What shall we do with the ark of the LORD?" they asked. "Tell us how we should send it back to its place" (6:2).

Their own "spiritual leaders" believed they needed to placate "this god" by sending gifts with the ark, which indicates the impact God's judgment had on the whole nation. Motivated by the superstition that permeated their own pagan religion, they told the Philistine leaders to mold five golden images that looked like the tumors God had sent their way and to also mold five golden rats that symbolized the hoards of field mice that had devoured their crops. The number five in both instances represented the five major Philistine cities (6:17) and the five rulers of these cities (6:18).

Hardening Their Hearts

In spite of the fact that the Philistine rulers recognized the supernatural nature of what had happened, when they faced the reality of not only being forced to return the ark to Israel but to send a "guilt offering" as well, their pride took over—

which always leads to a hardened heart! Recognizing what was happening, the "priests" and "diviners" challenged these political leaders to remember what happened to Pharaoh in Egypt so many years before. "Why do you harden your hearts as the Egyptians and Pharaoh did?" they asked. "When he [Israel's God] treated them harshly, did they not send the Israelites out so they could go on their way?" (6:6).

The very fact that the religious leaders among the Philistines remembered these plagues and catastrophes—even centuries later—demonstrates the incredible impact these miraculous events had on people beyond the confines of Egypt itself. Now they were attempting to get this message across to their own political leaders by reminding them of Pharaoh's response to God's judgments.

Hedging Their Bet

The Philistine rulers evidently wanted some verification from their own spiritual leaders that their suggestions were the right thing to do. Though convinced in their own minds, the religious leaders offered a "miraculous plan" of their own (1 Sam. 6:7–9). But they "hedged their bet" and told the Philistine rulers to select two cows that had just given birth. They were to remove their calves, hitch the cows to a cart loaded with the ark and the "guilt offering" gifts, and point these two animals in the direction of Beth Shemesh—a city that was set aside for the priests in Israel. If the cows, who had never been trained to pull a cart, proceeded toward this city, they could be sure that these plagues resulted because of a supernatural judgment. If the cows refused to leave their calves, they could be certain that they had simply experienced a natural disaster—a freak of nature.

Another Miracle

This was an unusual test. Anyone who has worked with cattle, or animals in general, knows exactly what would happen under normal circumstances. These "mothers" would never have left their newborns. They would have refused to move or more likely would have instinctively turned and headed for the stalls where the calves had been penned up. My father was a dairy farmer, and as a young man I remember getting into serious trouble with a mother cow when I even dared to touch her newborn. If I hadn't turned and high-tailed it in the other direction, I could have been mauled.

To say the least, these "spiritual leaders" definitely protected themselves. It's clear that some of the Philistine rulers —like Pharaoh—had hardened their hearts and were trying to convince the priests that the horrible and awesome things that had happened were accidental and unrelated to the ark of God. Perhaps they had threatened them in some way if they were giving bad advice.

To protect themselves, the priests evidently offered this unusual "way out" if they were wrong. The facts are, it was a rather safe test! From a human point of view, these animals would have never left their young. But to everyone's surprise, they miraculously turned away from their newborn calves and headed straight for Beth Shemesh—never turning "to the right or to the left" (6:10–12). Unknown to the Philistines, however, this miraculous event had nothing to do with their "gods" or their "magicians."

Rather, it was another act of grace and mercy on the part of Jehovah. He was sending them another message that He was the one true God.

The Ark Is Back

Imagine the emotional reactions of the Israelites who lived in Beth Shemesh when they looked up and saw this strange but wonderful sight—two cows pulling a cart with the ark of God perched on top. Predictably, "they rejoiced" (6:13). In fact, to express their thanksgiving to God they chopped up the cart and offered the two cows as a sacrifice to the Lord (6:14).

After watching these things in amazement, "the five rulers of the Philistines. . . . then returned that same day to Ekron" (6:16). Though they certainly must have breathed a sigh of relief, they must have also scratched their heads in wonderment as they watched the Israelites slaughter the cows, chop up the cart, and offer a sacrifice to the God who had delivered them from Egyptian bondage. Unfortunately, they still hardened their hearts and refused to turn from their pagan ways and bow their own knees before the Lord of heaven and earth.

God wasn't through teaching Israel some dramatic lessons regarding His holiness. At some point during all of this unusual activity, seventy men in Beth Shemesh became curious and took some unusual liberties with the ark (6:19). They opened the lid and looked inside—only to be struck dead! Predictably, the rest of the people in Beth Shemesh were terribly frightened. They were so fearful of God's holy presence that they had the ark transported to Kiriath Jearim (6:20–21).

Twenty Years Later

Two decades passed after the ark was moved to this new location. All during this period, the children of Israel continued to live in Philistine bondage.

A Cry for Help

In spite of the fact that the ark of God had been returned, most of the Israelites continued to follow their own way. However, some in Israel "mourned" over their condition and "sought after the Lord" (7:2). Evidently, as more and more of God's people became incredibly unhappy with their plight, they intensified their cry for help. Finally, Samuel—who was also twenty years older since Israel's humiliating defeat at the hands of the Philistines—responded to the people's plea with these words: "'If you are returning to the LORD with all your hearts, then rid yourselves of the foreign gods and the Ashtoreths and commit yourselves to the LORD and serve him only, and he will deliver you out of the hand of the Philistines'" (7:3).

Samuel's Mature Perspective

All through chapter seven you'll notice a great contrast to Samuel's reactions two decades earlier. First of all, his response indicates that something has transpired in his own life. Obviously, he had learned a lot about doing God's work in God's way. When he had encouraged Israel to go up and fight with the Philistines, he was probably a young teenager. Though he had been receiving direct messages from God, he stepped out on his own when he issued an order that turned out to be an error in judgment that was catastrophic! But as God does so often, He can take mistakes (and even evil actions) and make it work for good—which is beautifully illustrated in the life of Joseph (Gen. 50:19–20) and reinforced in the New Testament when Paul wrote these words to the Romans: "And we know that in all things God works for the good of those who love Him, who have been called according to his purpose" (Rom. 8:28).

This great truth in no way excuses Samuel's youthful error, but God used this mistake to get his and all Israel's attention. How could he ever forget that thirty-four thousand men lost their lives in battle and the Philistines captured the ark of God!

One of Samuel's greatest lessons was that if Israel were to defeat the Philistines and extricate themselves from this bondage, they needed to forsake foreign gods and seek the Lord's help. Samuel learned a lesson that was indelibly impressed on his heart and mind. That impression is reflected in his response to Israel's plea.

Straddling the Fence

In spite of all the children of Israel had gone through—including the miraculous way God forced the Philistines to return the ark to their own cities—many still continued to worship false gods. This explains why Jehovah God turned a deaf ear to their emotional pain for twenty years. They wanted God's help, but they weren't willing to forsake their idolatry and their sinful and worldly lifestyles.

It's amazing how long it took the children of Israel to get the message that God delivered to Joshua centuries before. Deliverance and success was dependent upon obedience to God's eternal laws (Josh. 1:7–8). As long as they worshiped false gods or even "straddled the fence," God would not grant them victory over their enemies.

Seeking God's Help

Samuel's message to Israel was very similar to Joshua's, which he had delivered after they had miraculously conquered great portions of the land of Palestine. "'Now then,' said Joshua, 'throw away the foreign gods that are among you and yield your hearts to the LORD, the God of Israel.' And the people said to Joshua, 'We will serve the LORD our God and obey him'" (Josh. 24:23–24).

Samuel's words that day not only reflect Joshua's charge to Israel hundreds of years before, but the peoples' response is almost identical. In fact, their actions speak louder than their words. We read: "So the Israelites put away their Baals and Ashtoreths, and served the LORD only" (1 Sam. 7:4).

When Israel destroyed their false gods, Samuel took the next strategic step. He asked the children of Israel to gather together at Mizpah so he could pray for them (7:5). Pragmatically speaking, this city was a strategic location for Israel to launch a military campaign against the Philistines. But more so, what happened there would enable the Philistines to observe Israel's *spiritual* preparation to go to war.

In addition to offering prayers for help through Samuel, their mediator, the people "drew water and poured it out before the LORD. On that day they fasted and there they confessed 'we have sinned against the Lord'" (7:6).

Pouring water on the ground symbolized their horrible distress. Years later, King David used the same metaphor when he cried out to God in the midst of his own distress: "I am poured out like water, and all my bones are out of joint. My heart has turned to wax; it has melted away within me" (Ps. 22:14).

Fasting before the Lord indicates their humiliation and willingness to sacrifice their own physical needs to devote time to seeking God's face. Again, David illustrates this same attitude and practice when he was betrayed by his own people. In despair he cried out to God: "They repay me evil for good and leave my soul forlorn. Yet when they were ill, I put on sackcloth and humbled myself with fasting" (Ps. 35:12–13a).

What a contrast from twenty years earlier. Believing they would be victorious, the leaders in Israel had sent their army into battle thinking God would help them win, even though they were involved in horrible idolatry and immorality. What a presumptuous and prideful attitude! But now, they humbled themselves before the Lord, confessed their sins, and sought God's help. Two decades had not blurred their memories regarding their horrible defeat the last time they went up against the Philistines and why it happened.

Victory at Last

Israel gathered at Mizpah in order to seek the Lord—not to war against the Philistines as they had done at Ebenezer two decades earlier (1 Sam. 4:1). Even though they knew that Mizpah was a strategic battle location, this was not their primary purpose in being there. They came because of Samuel's order to *pray, fast* and *confess their sins.*

As before, the Philistines were ready—assuming they were about to be attacked. Twenty years had not blurred their own memories of Israel's previous strategy against them.

Consequently, they assembled to attack Israel, creating intense fear among God's people (7:7).

At this point, we see another contrast! The children of Israel realized they could not defeat their enemies in their own strength. They pleaded with Samuel to keep praying for them: "'Do not stop crying out to the LORD our God for us, that he may rescue us from the hand of the Philistines'" (7:8).

Samuel responded to Israel's cry for help. As a teenager, he had simply issued an order to go into battle against the Philistines. This time, however, he offered a sacrifice—a "suckling lamb"—and "cried out to the Lord on Israel's behalf" (7:9).

Mercifully—but not surprisingly—the Lord responded to Samuel's intercession and granted Israel a great victory. They were now *doing things God's way!* His presence was very evident. We read that "The Lord thundered with loud thunder against the Philistines and threw them into such a panic that they were routed before the Israelites" (7:10).

Following Israel's victory over the Philistines, Samuel placed a stone "between Mizpah and Shem" and called it Ebenezer, which means—"thus far has the LORD helped us" (7:12). With this act of worship, Samuel was also sending Israel a message. They had defeated the Philistines because they *had done things God's way.*

Yes, the "Ebenezer" message was clear. Should they forsake God and do things their way, He would also forsake them and once again allow them to go back into bondage. Fortunately, for years to come they followed God's will, and the Lord granted them a certain amount of freedom from the Philistines throughout Samuel's judgeship.

Becoming God's Man Today

Principles to Live By

This is a powerful passage of Scripture with some very practical lessons for all of us. Following are some specific principles that we can apply in our own lives today in a variety of situations:

Principle 1. We cannot expect God to answer our prayers, reveal His presence, and give us victory over Satan when we are "straddling the fence"—walking with one foot in the world of idolatry and worldliness and the other in the spiritual realm.

How many people do you know who claim to be Bible-believing Christians and yet have one foot in the world and the other in the realm of biblical truth? Their divided loyalties are not a matter of ignorance regarding what God says, but rather a deliberate decision to "straddle the fence." They want to "have their cake and eat it too."

As we've seen, this kind of lifestyle is nothing new in the history of God's people. As Christians, however, we should know better and live better. We have the history of Israel—both their successes and failures—clearly described for us in the Old Testament. Furthermore, we have the history of the church in the New Testament, and if we truly know the Lord Jesus Christ as personal Savior, we have the Holy Spirit dwelling within us who is always ready to enable and empower us to live a dedicated, consistent Christian life.

Obedience and Answered Prayer

James made it clear who God hears. Using the prophet Elijah as a dynamic illustration, he wrote: "The prayer of a righteous man is powerful and effective" (James 5:16b).

Peter made the same point but applied it in a special way to Christian husbands. After instructing Christian wives regarding the way they should live with their unsaved husbands, he directed some powerful words to Christian men: "Husbands, in the same way be considerate as you live with your wives, and treat them with respect as the weaker partner and as heirs with you of the gracious gift of life, *so that nothing will hinder your prayers*" (1 Pet. 3:7).

A Powerful and Practical Message

I'll never forget hearing Chuck Swindoll speak on this verse one day in chapel at Dallas Theological Seminary. I was a relatively new professor at the time and I was jolted by his message. In essence, Peter was saying that the degree to which God answers my prayers depends on the degree to which I love my wife as Christ loved me (Eph. 5:25).

This truth, of course, should jolt every man. But it applies to all Christians who want God's blessings yet refuse to "play the game" according to God's rules. To do otherwise is to attempt to manipulate God—to get the sovereign Lord of the universe to play according *to our rules!* It just doesn't work that way—and understandably so. The principle we've just stated is clear in both the Old and New Testaments.

Principle 2. When we serve the Lord with all our hearts and turn from our sinful behavior, God will respond to fervent prayers and enable us to take our "stand against the devil's schemes" (Eph. 6:11).

This principle underscores the positive dimension regarding answered prayer. God loves to hear His children pray, and He loves to respond when we ask for help. He has promised victory over our archenemy, Satan, when we "put on the full armor of God" (Eph. 6:11).

In this Ephesian passage, Paul reminded us that "our struggle is not against flesh and blood, but against the rulers, against the authorities, against the powers of this dark world and against the spiritual forces of evil in the heavenly realms" (6:12). This is why we must "put on the *full* armor of God" (6:13). When we do, we will "be able to stand our ground."

One important piece of armor includes "the breastplate of righteousness," which represents not just our position in Christ because of faith but also our ongoing relationship with Christ because of obedience.

Paul concludes this marvelous metaphorical passage with a very literal statement. Once we've put on God's armor, we are *then* to "pray in the Spirit on all occasions with all kinds of prayers and requests" (6:18).

Principle 3. Though we have access to God's heart directly through our great High Priest, Jesus Christ, we also need the prayers of godly people who will intercede for us.

One Mediator

In the true sense of the word, we do not need a human priest like Moses or Samuel to intercede for us before God. Today, there is only "one mediator between God and men, the man Christ Jesus, who gave himself as a ransom for all men" (1 Tim. 2:5–6). He is our great High Priest who enables us to "approach the throne of grace with confidence, so that we may receive mercy and find grace to help us in our time of need" (Heb. 4:16).

Mutual Intercessors

On the other hand, each of us also needs the prayers of God's people—not to be our "go-between" but to join us in prayer as all of us offer prayers for one another to God through Jesus Christ. This is why James also wrote: "Therefore confess your sins to each other and pray for each other so that you may be healed. The prayer of a righteous man is powerful and effective" (James 5:16).

To refuse to ask others to pray for us is often a mark of pride. We're fearful that people will think less of us if we admit we need help from others within the body of Jesus Christ. When we're tempted to think this way, we need to remind ourselves of what Jesus said to His disciples: "'Again, I tell you that if two of you on earth agree about anything you ask for, it will be done for you by my Father in heaven. For where two or three come together in my name, there I am with them'" (Matt. 18:19–20).

*Principle 4. We should never fail to honor God
and give Him the glory for our successes, victories,
and accomplishments.*

When God gave the children of Israel victory over the Philistines, Samuel erected a stone and "named it Ebenezer." He wanted to remind Israel in days to come that it was the Lord who had helped them win this great victory.

As I reflected on this marvelous example in Samuel's life, my mind went back to a song I learned and often sang as a young Christian. The title of the song is "Come, Thou Fount of Every Blessing" and the second verse reads as follows:

> Here I raise mine Ebenezer;
> Hither by Thy help I'm come;
> And I hope, by Thy good pleasure,
> Safely to arrive at home.
> Jesus sought me when a stranger,
> Wand'ring from the fold of God;
> He, to rescue me from danger,
> Interposed His precious blood.

I must admit I didn't really understand what Robert Robinson really meant when he penned these words. However, after studying this Old Testament story, it's clear that this author had bathed his heart in the great truths that emerge from this passage and interpreted these truths in the light of the New Testament. In essence, Robinson was saying that he too wanted to be reminded that only God's grace made it possible for him, not only to become a Christian, but to be at this particular point in his Christian walk. And it was his hope in Christ that would enable him to "press on toward the goal to win the prize for which God" had "called" him "heavenward in Christ Jesus" (Phil. 3:14).

Personalizing These Principles

The following are four statements followed by a scale from one to ten. As you read each statement, circle the number that best describes your walk with God. This will help you determine the extent to which you are doing things God's way or your own way.

1. As a Christian, I am keeping in step with the Holy Spirit, reflecting His fruit in my life (Gal. 5:22–25).

   1   2   3   4   5   6   7   8   9   10

   Never   Always

2. As a Christian, I love the Lord my God with all my heart, with all my soul, and with all my mind.

   1   2   3   4   5   6   7   8   9   10

   Never   Always

3. As a Christian, I rely on other believers to pray for me so that I might live in the good, acceptable, and perfect will of God (Rom. 12: 2).

   1   2   3   4   5   6   7   8   9   10

   Never   Always

4. As a Christian, I continually thank God and give Him the glory for the victories and accomplishments in my life.

   1   2   3   4   5   6   7   8   9   10

   Never   Always

Set a Goal

As you reflect on the results of this exercise, what one goal do you need to set for your life? Ask the Holy Spirit to direct you in this exercise.

Memorize the Following Scripture

> *Be very careful, then, how you live—not as unwise but as wise, making the most of every opportunity, because the days are evil. Therefore do not be foolish, but understand what the Lord's will is.*
> Ephesians 5:15–17

Growing Together

The following questions are designed for small group discussion:

1. Would you be willing to share your own personal journey in your Christian faith? Has there ever been a time in your life where you have "straddled the fence," experiencing a broken relationship with God? How did this affect your prayer life and your relationships with other Christians?

2. When did you learn to serve the Lord with all your heart and with all your soul? What do you do when you fail to practice this greatest of all commandments?

3. Would you share a prayer that was answered as a result of sharing your needs with other believers?

4. How do you consistently remind yourself to give God the honor and glory for the successes, victories, and accomplishments in your life?

5. In what way can we pray for you personally?

Chapter 9

Abusing and Misusing Freedom
Read 1 Samuel 7:15–8:22

*M*ore than we realize, God has given all of us a great deal of freedom to make decisions, to make choices, to be creative and innovative. However, He has also established boundaries to enable us to live within "his good, pleasing and perfect will" (Rom. 12:2). God even gives us freedom to operate outside of His divine guidelines, but if we do, we'll ultimately suffer the consequences. We can abuse and misuse the freedom God has given us by making self-centered decisions. The children of Israel learned this lesson the hard way, and in this chapter we'll learn what happens when we make choices that take us out of God's perfect will. We'll also learn how to avoid Israel's mistakes.

Back Home Again

To this point in his life, Samuel had served as a prophet in Israel, receiving direct messages from God and communicating those messages to God's people—even at a very young age (3:19–20). However, over the years God set the stage for Samuel to assume a new position. After he had led Israel to national repentance (1 Sam. 7:6) and to a miraculous victory over the Philistines, Samuel became an official judge (7:15).[1]

A Traveling "Pastor"

At this time Samuel was a relatively young man, but from this point forward he continued as judge over Israel "all the days of his life." He carried out his responsibilities as a traveling "pastor." We read that "from year to year he went on a circuit from Bethel to Gilgal to Mizpah, judging Israel in all those places" (7:16). But he always returned to his childhood home in Ramah (see fig. 9.1).

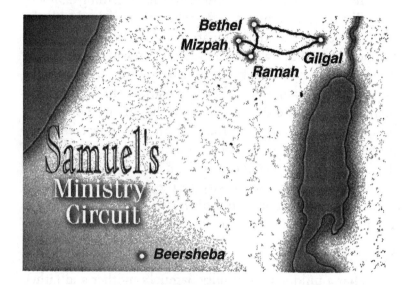

Figure 9.1

Once the ark was captured and following Eli's death, Samuel evidently moved back home to live with his parents. The tabernacle was probably destroyed by the Philistines. Since the high priest was dead, as well as his sons, there would be no reason for young Samuel to remain in Shiloh. Furthermore, he would be terribly traumatized over what had happened.

You can imagine how thrilled his mother, Hannah, must have been to see her son return home and stay with them during the twenty-year period Israel suffered under Philistine rule and domination. And once he became an official judge, Samuel continued to make Ramah his "home base." He continued to pray and intercede for Israel and to sacrifice to the Lord (7:17).

Some believe that he probably served as high priest as well as judge, making circuit trips each year to Bethel, Gilgal and Mizpah, always returning to the place where he was born.

A Secure Haven

Though we're not given specific details regarding Samuel's home life once he returned to Ramah, we can fill in the blanks with some sanctified imagination. We're not told when Samuel married nor whom he married, but when he returned home he may have still been in his teen years. For the next two decades, Hannah had her boy back—which, from her point of view, more than made up for her sacrifice of leaving him to assist Eli in the tabernacle at Shiloh. In fact, this was probably a secure haven for Samuel, following the terrible defeat Israel had experienced at the hands of the Philistines. Knowing this man's sensitivity to the Lord, he must have spent many days pouring out his heart and soul before God and his parents over what had happened.

Spiritual Growth

What a unique opportunity Samuel's mother and father had to comfort and reassure him that he was indeed a special young man in God's sight. Being a normal teenager, his mind must have been filled with serious doubts about his religious faith, especially in view of the tragedy he had witnessed in Shiloh. Samuel probably learned his greatest spiritual lessons during this twenty-year period. Eli may have mentored him in the basics of temple worship, but it was his parents who eventually had the opportunity to nurture him in his personal relationship with God and to encourage him to carry out his great calling in life.

By the time Samuel was in his mid-thirties or early forties, he emerged as a mature leader who was destined to lead the children of Israel out of idolatry and to victory over the Philistines when they went into a period of mourning and "sought after the

Lord" (7:2). As we've seen in the previous chapter, Samuel's approach to confronting Philistine bondage and the sins in Israel the second time around was 180 degrees different from the way he had handled this spiritual challenge two decades earlier.

Decades Later

Throughout Samuel's lifetime, "the hand of the Lord was against the Philistines" (7:13). Under his wise leadership the children of Israel prospered and experienced protection from their enemies. But eventually all was not well in Samuel's own household.

When Samuel became an old man, somewhere between 65 and 70 years of age, he experienced keen disappointment. It's a sad and heartrending commentary. Any God-fearing father who has attempted to serve the Lord, only to see some of his children walk away from God, can identify with Samuel's experience. We read that when he "grew old, he appointed" his sons, Joel and Abijah, "as judges for Israel" (8:1). However, they did not follow Samuel's example. Rather, "they turned aside after dishonest gain and accepted bribes and perverted justice" (8:3).

Two Important Questions

What happened to Samuel's sons raises two very important questions:

- Were Samuel's sons guilty of these sins when he appointed them as his assistants to help him judge Israel?
- Furthermore, did he rebuke his sons when he found out about their evil deeds?

We're not given detailed answers to these questions in the biblical record. However, based on the overall story of Samuel's life, we can come up with some very satisfactory answers.

Vivid Memories

I'd like to speak to the second question first. It seems highly improbable that this prophet committed the same sins as Eli since his first message from God as a young boy in the tabernacle at Shiloh detailed the judgment God was going to bring on Eli and why it was going to happen. How could he forget the details of that revelation—that God was going to judge Eli's "family forever because of the sin he knew about"; that his sons had "made themselves contemptible, and he failed to restrain them" (3:13)? Furthermore, Samuel saw this prophecy come true when Hophni and Phinehas both died in battle "on the same day" (2:34; 4:11).

It was because of Samuel's word that all of this happened (4:1). Though I personally believe this young prophet made an error in judgment in sending Israel into battle against the Philistines, God in His sovereignty used this tragic mistake to carry out His judgment against Eli's household. How could Samuel forget these events and make the same mistake as Eli? Frankly, I think he remembered every detail until the day he died. Furthermore, how could he forget what happened to the ark of God and the place of worship at Shiloh?

Departure from God's Will

This leads us back to the first question. Were Samuel's sons guilty of these sins when he appointed them as his assistants to help judge Israel? I don't believe so. It seems Joel and Abijah departed from the will of God *after* Samuel appointed them as judges.

Note two things in the text that support this conclusion. First, "they served at Beersheba" (8:2b), a city located nearly fifty miles south of Ramah (see fig. 9.2). This was a long distance in those days, which would make it very difficult for Samuel to monitor his sons' activities and to hold them accountable. Considering the fact that some spiritual leaders today get away with horrible sins right under our noses certainly makes it

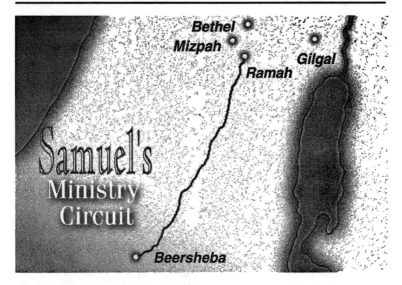

Figure 9.2

understandable why Samuel wasn't cognizant of what Joel and Abijah were doing until he received a report from the elders of Israel.

Second, notice that the flow of the written account also suggests this conclusion. We read that "his sons did not walk in His ways. *They turned aside* after dishonest gain and accepted bribes and perverted justice" (8:3, emphasis mine). In other words, when Joel and Abijah were "on their own" with full responsibility to make decisions, they yielded to the temptation to be dishonest and to pad their own pockets. They betrayed their father and the God they were serving.

That this should happen should not surprise us. I've worked with men and women for many years—people whose hearts were right with God. In some instances, I discipled these people and saw their spiritual growth over a period of years. They had my full trust and confidence—a primary reason they occupied significant positions of responsibility. Never in a million years would I guess they would turn aside to do evil in the sight of the Lord. But they did—within an environment that was very conducive to maintaining moral and ethical integrity, including a system of accountability. To this very day I find it difficult to believe they betrayed and deceived me as well as their fellow pastors and the total congregation. But in retrospect, I can see how it can happen to some of God's most dedicated Christians—men and women who lower their guard and fail to continue to put on the full armor of God.

A Sinful Environment

We must remember that Samuel's sons grew up in an environment that was far more conducive to sin than ours, which makes it more understandable as to why Joel and Abijah got caught up in sinful actions. Though the children of Israel had turned from false gods at this point in their lives, they were never known to be free from attitudes and actions that violated the law of God. Even when they worshiped the one true God, they often violated His moral and ethical codes. Rather than correct these problems in Israel—as a good judge should do—Samuel's sons committed the same sins they were supposed to confront and correct. Though this does not excuse their behavior, it helps us to understand why it happened.

A Painful Confrontation

Imagine Samuel's emotional turmoil and pain when "all the elders of Israel gathered together" and confronted him at Ramah, saying, "You are old, and your sons do not walk in your ways; now appoint a king to lead us, such as all the other nations have" (8:4–5).

We're not told what Samuel had to say about his sons, but again we can read between the lines. He was obviously disappointed and felt betrayed, but as a leader in Israel he had to address a much larger issue and problem: the elders had asked for a king. We're told that he was "displeased" and true man of

God that he was, he went to prayer (8:6). He asked God for wisdom and direction.

Samuel was obviously surprised at the Lord's response. God told him to listen to everything the elders were saying, which would include the report about his sons. In other words, God affirmed that Joel and Abijah had indeed been guilty as accused. But more specifically, God dealt with their request for a king. Listen to the Lord's answer: "'It is not you they have rejected, but they have rejected me as their king. As they have done from the day I brought them up out of Egypt until this day, forsaking me and serving other gods, so they are doing to you. Now listen to them; but warn them solemnly and let them know what the king who will reign over them will do'" (8:7–9).

The Lord's answer gives us some additional insights. Samuel felt hurt and rejected. He had been accused of being too old, which implies he had lost touch with what was happening, even in his own family. Rather than giving him a chance to correct the problem, the elders asked for a king—a direct inference that he could no longer lead effectively. In view of all that Samuel had done for Israel, it's understandable why he felt rejected and unappreciated.

A Self-centered Request

At this point in the dramatic story, we understand more fully why God was so displeased with Israel's demand for a king. It was not the request per se, since God had given them the freedom to ask for a king in the laws outlined by Moses in the Book of Deuteronomy (Deut. 17:14–15a). However, when the elders of Israel approached Samuel, their request was self-centered and carnal. Years of freedom from Philistine bondage and success as a nation had blurred their memories and led them to think only of themselves and the way things were done in the pagan world around them.

What a contrast from the way the leaders in Israel had responded years earlier! At that time, they put away their "foreign gods" and "served the LORD only" (7:3–4). They fasted and prayed, confessing their sins (7:6). When they went into battle against the Philistines, they pleaded with Samuel to cry out to the Lord for them so that they might have victory (7:8). God was in the center of their lives. But now there was no hint of asking Samuel to determine God's will regarding a king. There is no reference to prayer and no evidence of humility. They wanted what they wanted—and they wanted it immediately.

A Solemn Warning

God told Samuel to warn Israel of what would happen when they had a human king ruling over them. Their freedom to choose a king would eliminate many freedoms they now enjoyed. More tragically, the way they were using their freedom had offended the Lord who had delivered them again and again from bondage—a very dangerous position to be in. When we "bite the hand that feeds us," we're asking for trouble—especially when it's God's hand!

As a faithful prophet, Samuel conveyed "all the words" the Lord had told him to communicate to Israel (8:10). Many of their sons would have to serve the king—in many ways (8:12). Their daughters would have to do the same (8:13). The king would impose taxes on them that would be an incredible burden (8:14–17). The day would come when they would "cry out for relief," but the Lord would not answer them (8:18).

Hardened Hearts

Even though the children of Israel knew Samuel was a true prophet of God who always spoke the truth, not withholding anything God revealed to him, they rejected this old sage's message. They "refused to listen" to God's Word through Samuel. "'No!' they said. 'We want a king over us. Then we will be like all the other nations, with a king to lead us and to go out before us and fight our battles'" (8:19–20).

At this moment, the leaders in Israel were not only using the legitimate freedom God had given them, but they were using this freedom to walk out of the will of God! They had hardened their hearts. As a result, God allowed them to seal their own fate. Sadly, we read, "When Samuel heard all that the people said, he repeated it before the LORD. The LORD answered, 'Listen to them and give them a king'" (8:21).

As painful as it was, Samuel resigned himself to what was happening before his very eyes. Consequently, he "closed the meeting" and sent everyone "back to his town" (8:23). Samuel knew he could not change their minds. They had not rejected him, but God.

Becoming God's Man Today

Principles to Live By

Principle 1. Though God promises never to leave us nor forsake us, as parents we have no guarantee that our children will never make decisions that are out of God's will once they're old enough to function on their own.

I wish I could point all of us to some Scripture that will guarantee that we can do everything perfectly as parents. The fact is that parenting is an aspect of Christian living—and none of us live perfect Christian lives. If we could, we'd already be completely like Jesus Christ in all aspects of our lives. That won't happen until we are with Christ. Then we'll be like Him since we'll see Him as He is.

I also wish I could point you to a Scripture that guarantees that if we do everything right—which is impossible—that our children will never depart from the will of God, particularly once they grow up and leave the home environment. Even while they live with us, our "home is not an island."

Obviously, we should do everything we can to be consistent role models—which is foundational. We should teach our children God's Word, both by example and precept. We should do all we can to protect them from evil influences. We should also pray and guide our children to attend a church where God's Word is taught and where they can become a part of a functioning body of believers that is "building itself up in love." However, there will come a time when our children are on their own. At this point, our primary source of hope is to pray that they'll make God-centered decisions in all aspects of their lives and when they fail the Lord—and they will—that they'll turn back to God.

Understanding Their Natural Bent

One of the most reassuring verses is in Proverbs: "Train a child in the way he should go, and when he is old he will not turn from it" (22:6).

Unfortunately, this does not guarantee a positive result in all situations, but it is very encouraging—especially if we understand what this Scripture means. If we train up our children according to their "unique ways"—according to their natural bent and the way God has created them—our children will respect us, love us, and respond to us. Put another way, if we are understanding and sensitive to their psychological make-up, we set the stage for teachability and influence. They will never be able to forget what we've taught them and modeled with our own lives.

Principle 2. We must always be on guard against losing perspective, forgetting what God has done for us, ignoring His Word, hardening our hearts and making our own self-centered decisions.

This is one of the greatest lessons we can learn from the children of Israel. We need not fail like they did. We have a choice, based on a great deal of knowledge. We know what it means to love God with all our hearts and to communicate that love to our children—or we can choose to disobey the Lord and fail to practice what we preach. When we do, we'll suffer the consequences in our own lives and in the lives of our children. When we follow God's principles, we'll be able to defeat Satan in our own lives and in the lives of our children.

Principle 3. God has given us unusual freedom to make decisions and choices and to be creative and innovative; however, He wants us to function within His divine guidelines, having pure motives and proper heart attitudes.

This is a very positive principle. Think of the freedoms God gives us: where to work, where to worship, where to live, whom to marry, where to go on vacation, where to go to school, etc. All of these decisions, however, should be made in the light of the principles and guidelines in the Word of God. For example, we're given freedom to marry; but if we want to be within God's divine guidelines, we should marry a Christian. To be unequally yoked in this most intimate of all relationships will lead to tension, confusion, and a home where we cannot even agree on what we should teach our children.

Remember, too, that God gives us freedom to make deliberate choices to walk out of His will in many other aspects of life, following the acts of the sinful nature (Gal. 5:19–21). But we mustn't "be deceived." For example, if we choose to deliberately make moral choices that are out of the will of God—including illegitimate sexual relationships—we'll "reap what we sow" (Gal. 6:7). If we choose to be unethical, we'll also "reap what we sow." If we're selfish and arrogant, we'll "reap what we sow" in that area of our lives.

There's also good news. If we present our bodies to Jesus Christ and renew our minds—not conforming our lives to the world's system but allowing ourselves to be transformed into the image of Jesus Christ—we'll discover and enjoy the wonderful, good, acceptable, and perfect will of God (Rom. 12:1–2). There's no place so comforting and reassuring than when we are walking worthy of that great calling we have in Christ (Eph. 4:1).

Personalizing These Principles

Following are some questions to help you practice these principles in your own life. Read them carefully and prayerfully, asking the Holy Spirit to open your heart to His Word:

1. Do you feel guilty because of what has happened to your children? Are you punishing yourself for your parental mistakes?

   If you answer "yes" to either of these questions, confess any sins to God and accept His forgiveness (1 John 1:9). Then do what you can to change things. For example, ask forgiveness from your children. But once you've taken these steps, you must go on with your life. Change what you can and accept what you cannot change!

2. What steps have you taken to remind yourself of what God has done for you in the past? What are you doing to be on guard when temptations come to ignore God's Word and go your own way?

   If your heart is the least bit hard, confess that sin to God and ask Him to help you respond to His will.

3. How well do you understand God's will as outlined in the Word of God? Are you making choices and decisions based on His eternal principles and guidelines?

   Remember that what is often taught and lived in our culture is very frequently diametrically opposed to God's plan for our lives.

Set a Goal

As a result of this exercise in applying these principles to your life, what one need has the Holy Spirit brought to your attention? Based on this insight and conviction, set a personal goal:

_____

_____

_____

_____

Memorize the Following Scripture

You, my brothers, were called to be free. But do not use your freedom to indulge the sinful nature; rather, serve one another in love.
GALATIANS 5:13

Growing Together

The following questions are designed for small group study.

1. What have you learned from the Word of God and other mature Christians that has helped you to be a better parent?

2. What have you learned from your own failure as a parent? And what have you done to correct these failures? What has been the result?

3. How have you overcome guilt and self-punishment, particularly regarding parental mistakes that have caused your children to walk out of the will of God?

4. What has encouraged you the most in fulfilling your parental role?

5. In what way can we pray for you specifically?

Chapter 10

God's Permissive Will
Read 1 Samuel 8:21–10:1

We've already noted that God gives us a great deal of freedom. All people can choose to accept His gift of salvation or
to reject it. As Christians, we can choose to walk in harmony
with His Holy Spirit or we can make decisions that are more
in harmony with "our sinful nature." When we choose to
make decisions that are selfish and self-centered, we've chosen
to leave God's "perfect will" and live in His "permissive
will"—and when we do, we'll suffer negative consequences.
We learn this lesson again and again from the nation of Israel.

An Intimate Conversation

Samuel was grieved that Israel's leaders had demanded a
king, but he reconciled himself to God's permissive will. After
all, God Himself had spelled out clearly what a king would
demand and the price they would have to pay, and Samuel had
"told all the words of the Lord to the people" (1 Sam. 8:10). Yet
they had hardened their hearts, knowing full well that for
years Samuel had always been completely open and truthful
with them regarding God's prophetic messages. But when
they rejected this message with an arrogant "no," stating that
they wanted to be like "all the other nations," Samuel communicated with the Lord what they had said.

Why did Samuel report Israel's words to God when He
already knew every detail of this dialogue? For one thing, we

have a glimpse into the intimate relationship Samuel had with Jehovah God. Like Moses, this old judge and prophet conversed directly with the Lord, receiving messages and giving messages. Could it be that God designed these intimate conversations more for Samuel than for anyone else? In the midst of this crisis, he needed this kind of intimate communication to soothe his troubled soul and to assist him in carrying out his awesome responsibilities in Israel. God reassured Samuel that he was doing the "right thing" even though Israel was doing the "wrong thing."

"Give Them a King"

We must remember that asking for a king was not Israel's sin. Rather, God was displeased because the leaders in Israel wanted to put their trust in a man rather than in Him. If they had asked with pure hearts, they would have been in God's perfect will. However, they asked with impure motives that were selfish and sinful. Consequently, God told Samuel to give them what they wanted—a king (8:22). Rather than choosing God's "perfect will," they opted for His "permissive will"—even though they knew they and their children would suffer some very serious consequences.

"An Impressive Young Man"

At this point, we see an amazing aspect of God's divine nature. Even though Israel had chosen to deliberately disobey Him, the Lord did not forsake His people. In fact, He chose their king. Only a sovereign, all-knowing, and all-powerful God can do this sort of thing without contradicting Himself.

The man God chose was Saul. His father's name was Kish (9:1), a "man of standing" in the Benjamite community, which means he was well-known, respected, and a "man of means."

Kish's son, Saul, is described as "an impressive young man without equal," not only in the tribe of Benjamin but also "among the Israelites" (9:2). We're told specifically that he was a "head taller than any of the others." And being an outdoors man, Saul was literally "tall, dark, and handsome."

Some Lost Donkeys

As He so often does, God used human circumstances to achieve His divine purposes—in this instance, some "lost donkeys." We read: "Now the donkeys belonging to Saul's father Kish were lost, and Kish said to his son Saul, 'Take one of the servants with you and go and look for the donkeys'" (9:3).

Though I have never worked with donkeys, I have worked with a related species—mules. My own father had a pair—Jack and Jenny—and they were forever breaking through a fence or forcing their way through a gate and wandering off. I remember many days we got in our old '34 Ford truck back on the family farm in Indiana and headed off to look for Jack and Jenny! We usually found them on an old dirt road several miles from home, simply enjoying their freedom. But when they saw us coming, they hightailed it for home, with Dad and me following close behind in the old Ford truck. After several episodes it seemed to become a game!

Saul's task was more difficult. He and his servant literally searched "high and low" since they looked for these animals in a mountainous region (9:4). After three days (9:20), Saul began to worry that his father would shift his concern for the lost donkeys to a concern for a lost son and servant. "Come, let's go back," Saul said to his traveling companion, "or my father will stop thinking about the donkeys, and start worrying about us" (9:5).

Divine Orchestration

We're not told how Saul's servant knew that Samuel was coming to a nearby town (9.6).[1] Perhaps he had visited the night before to ask about the lost donkeys. Had anyone seen them? Predictably, someone may have suggested he talk with the "old seer" who was supposed to arrive the next day. If anyone could help them, certainly Samuel could. The town would be buzzing with excitement since it probably was a rare occasion for Samuel to visit in this part of Canaan. After all, he was Israel's judge and high priest, the man who resolved their social and political problems and also represented them before God.

Whatever the circumstances, Saul's servant believed he might have found a way to find the donkeys. "Let's go there now," he said to Saul with a sense of urgency. "Perhaps he will tell us what way to take" (9:6b).

Divine Appointments

Saul and his servant met Samuel coming their way as they entered the town (9:14). *In God's timing, Samuel had just arrived that very day.* The Lord, of course, was orchestrating all these circumstances to bring Samuel and Saul together. Unknown to Saul and his servant, God had already revealed to Samuel that he was about to meet the new king of Israel. More specifically, God had said, "About this time tomorrow I will send you a man from the land of Benjamin. Anoint him leader over my people Israel; he will deliver my people from the hand of the Philistines. I have looked upon my people, for their cry has reached me" (9:16).

Under Samuel's leadership, "the Philistines" had been "subdued and did not invade Israel's territory again" (7:13). God would use Saul, however, to lead Israel to go to war against the Philistines and to defeat them.

Isn't it amazing? In spite of Israel's rebellion against Him in wanting a king, God did not forsake His people and continued to hear their cry for help. He had orchestrated these "divine appointments." Only a loving and faithful God would do such a thing. Let it never be said that the Lord was ever unfair to Israel.

Some Shocking Statements

Saul had never met Samuel, or if he had, he didn't remember. We read, "Saul approached Samuel in the gateway and asked, 'Would you please tell me where the seer's house is?'" (9:18).

As prominent as Samuel was in Israel, not everyone knew who he was. This is understandable since he lived in Ramah and normally limited his travels to visiting only three other cities—Bethel, Gilgal, and Mizpah (see fig. 9.1). This unnamed town was probably some distance from Samuel's normal whereabouts.

Samuel identified himself and then shocked Saul with several statements. First, he instructed Saul to go up to the high place to join him in a meal—a high honor indeed. In fact, to go "before him" and "ahead" of a prophet was a violation of protocol. Only a very honored person would ever precede a prophet (9:19).

Second, Samuel read Saul's mind and revealed the concerns in his heart. He told Saul to stop worrying about the donkeys since they had already been found (9:20). Even if the servant had visited the city earlier and spread the word that they were looking for lost donkeys, how could Samuel have known they'd been found? Obviously, Samuel was verifying to Saul that he was indeed a seer—a true prophet of God.

Third, Samuel shared with Saul a startling fact when he said, "And to whom is all the desire of Israel turned, if not to you and all your father's family?"

Though Saul didn't discern at this moment what Samuel was really referring to—that he would be king—he knew instinctively that this was an unusual prophecy. Startled, he responded with sincerity and humility:

"But am I not a Benjamite, from the smallest tribe of Israel, and is not my clan the least of all the clans of the tribe of Benjamin? Why do you say such a thing to me?"

More Surprises

Apparently Samuel did not answer Saul's question. He simply directed him to meet him at the "high place." When they met the next day, Samuel escorted Saul and his servant into what must have been a relatively large hall where thirty other outstanding men in the community already were seated around a table. In an unusual act of honor, Samuel proceeded to seat both Saul and his servant at the head of the table (9:22).

Imagine Saul's surprise! It was strange enough for him to be treated this way, but to have his servant seated alongside him was another unusual departure from protocol.

But there were more surprises. Samuel had the cook bring a piece of meat he had already picked out for Saul prior to meeting him. Not only had Samuel selected this choice "leg of lamb," but he had already asked the cook to prepare it (9:23–24). Again, God enabled Samuel to verify his prophetic gift to prepare Saul for the most shocking news of all—that he was God's choice to be king over all Israel.

A Message from God

After they had dined together, Samuel invited Saul and his servant to be his guests where he was staying. Before retiring they talked "on the roof of his house" (9:25). We're not told the content of the conversation, but certainly Samuel said more things to prepare Saul for their conversation the next morning. At dawn, Samuel served as Saul's "alarm clock" and called to him on the rooftop where he and his servant had spent the night. "Get ready," Samuel said, "and I will send you on your way" (9:26).

As they walked together and came to the "edge of the town," Samuel asked for some time alone with Saul. He instructed him to send his servant on ahead, while they lingered behind. It was then that Samuel gave Saul "a message from God" (9:27).

We're not told specifically what this message was. Personally, I believe it was then that Samuel told Saul in no uncertain terms that God had chosen him to be king—in spite of Israel's unwillingness to do God's perfect will. I'm confident Samuel also told Saul about Israel's demand for a king and God's displeasure. Knowing Samuel, he would not have held back the whole truth. However, I'm also certain that Samuel reassured Saul that God would bless him and make him successful—regardless of Israel's self-centeredness and disobedience. In view of Saul's timid nature, he would certainly need this kind of affirmation.

A Divine Anointing

Whatever transpired between this old prophet and Saul during this private moment, the conversation ended when Samuel anointed Saul as King of Israel. We read, "Then Samuel took a flask of oil and poured it on Saul's head and kissed him, saying, 'Has not the LORD anointed you leader over his inheritance?'" (10:1).

Imagine how Saul felt! He must have been in total shock! He had gone out to try to find some lost donkeys and ended up being anointed as king of Israel! Like Joshua, who was appointed to replace Moses, his knees must have been trembling (Josh. 1:9).

Becoming God's Man Today

Principles to Live By

What can we learn from this tragic "historical moment" in Israel's life that dramatically changed their future? Following are some very important principles that are just as true today as they were three thousand years ago.

Principle 1. No person, no matter how qualified and wonderful his characteristics, should ever replace God in the hearts of God's people.

A Man Without Equal

I don't believe it is accidental that God chose a king for Israel with Saul's unique physical features. There was no man in all Israel who could compare with his external qualities. In a sense, he was a man without equal. His very physical presence gave people a sense of security as he towered above them.

The message seems clear. When the children of Israel asked for a man to serve as a king so they could be like the other nations around them, it was as if the Lord was saying, "I'll give you a man who is without equal. If you want to put your confidence in a human being, so be it!"

A Long-range Plan

Isn't it interesting that when Saul failed, God replaced him with a young man who certainly didn't compare with Saul in stature. Even as a youth, David went against a nine-foot giant named Goliath who towered above everyone in Israel—including Saul. David slew Goliath with a slingshot, crying out, "You come against me with sword and spear and javelin, but I come against you in the name of the LORD Almighty, the God of the armies of Israel, whom you have defied" (17:45).

Even when God chose Saul to be king, He had a "long-range plan." He anticipated using the Saul/David contrast to show His people that no man can take His place. But when a man loves God and puts Him first, the Lord can use him to accomplish great things—no matter what his age or size.

Even in the Christian community today, if we're not careful, we can worship men (and women), neglecting to keep our focus on God. And even Christian leaders must be careful that they do not foster and encourage this kind of behavior. No man should ever replace God in the hearts of people.

Principle 2. The only way to determine God's perfect will with an absolute sense of assurance and security is through the direct teachings of the Holy Scriptures.

As we've seen from our previous chapter, God gives us a great deal of freedom to make choices in order to function in life. However, He's established some very specific guidelines, directives, and principles to help us "test and approve what God's will is—his good, pleasing and perfect will" (Rom. 12:2).

For example, following that verse in Romans, God outlines very clearly what His perfect will is for every Christian:

- Do not think of yourself more highly than you ought, but rather think of yourself with sober judgment in accordance with the measure of faith God has given you (v. 3).
- Hate what is evil; cling to what is good (v. 9).
- Be devoted to one another in brotherly love. Honor one another above yourselves (v. 10).
- Be joyful in hope, patient in affliction, faithful in prayer (v. 12).
- Share with God's people who are in need. Practice hospitality (v. 13).
- Bless those who persecute you; bless and do not curse (v. 14).
- Live in harmony with one another. Do not be proud, but be willing to associate with people of low position. Do not be conceited (v. 16).
- Do not be overcome by evil, but overcome evil with good (v. 21).

These are simply a few selected directives from one chapter in the New Testament that outline God's perfect will for our lives. If we take these guidelines seriously, we'll have very little difficulty discerning God's perfect will in other areas of our lives.

Principle 3. When we choose God's permissive will rather than His perfect will—a choice which is usually based on self-centeredness and selfish desires—the negative consequences in our lives are usually commensurate with the degree of disobedience to God's clear message in the Word of God.

Let's take a couple of examples from the directives we've just outlined from Paul's letter to the Romans.

Attitudes Toward Others

God's perfect will is that I honor others above myself. However, God will permit me to honor myself above others! (12:10) But when I do, I'll suffer some negative consequences. I'll lose respect from others. Eventually, I'll lose respect for myself. I'll be a poor witness for Jesus Christ. Eventually, I'll get knocked off my perch since the Scriptures teach that "pride goes before destruction, a haughty spirit before a fall" (Prov. 16:18). Again, the negative consequences will normally correspond to the degree of self-centeredness involved and the extent to which this becomes a regular part of my lifestyle.

Generosity

It's God's perfect will that I be generous with my material possessions. I am to "share with God's people who are in need." I am to "practice hospitality" (Rom. 12:13).

Does God allow me to be selfish and stingy? Yes, He does. Sadly, there are more selfish Christians than unselfish Christians when it comes to giving. They are not living in God's "perfect will" but within His "permissive will." But when I am selfish, I will face negative consequences. I'll not experience the unique blessings that God bestows on generous Christians. And don't misunderstand, more important than material blessings are the spiritual blessings. For example, generous Christians experience a God-given joy that selfish Christians do not. In fact, selfish Christians don't even know what they're missing.

> *Principle 4. Though Christians reject God's perfect will and opt for His permissive will, the Lord never forsakes His children.*

When we choose to make decisions out of His perfect will, God will not forsake us, just as He did not forsake Israel. But we must not conclude that God's continual blessings and guidance are signs that He is pleased with what we've done.

For example, self-centered Christians are often very successful people—at least by the world's standards. Furthermore, there are a lot of selfish Christians who are not faithful and generous givers, but they're still making a lot of money. Unfortunately, it's easy to conclude that God is pleased with those decisions and choices.

Not so! Like Israel, we can be deceived. Because God is active in some areas of our lives does not mean that He is pleased with our behavior. Ultimately, we will suffer the negative consequences—if not in this life, in eternity. Paul stated that clearly in his letter to the Corinthians—a group of Christians that were definitely living out of His perfect will. He said that some of them would "be saved, but only as one escaping through the flames" (1 Cor. 3:15). Even though these Christians had eternal life, when they came face to face with Jesus Christ in eternity, they would have no rewards to present to Him.

Personalizing These Principles

Use the following questions and evaluation scales to help you apply these biblical principles. Circle the appropriate numbers.

1. To what extent have I replaced God with other human beings—my spouse, my family, a friend, a pastor?

Never   Much

1   2   3   4   5   6   7

2. To what extent have I failed to search the Scriptures to discover God's perfect will for my life?

Never   Much

1   2   3   4   5   6   7

3. To what extent am I making decisions and life choices that are out of God's perfect will?

Never   Much

1   2   3   4   5   6   7

4. To what extent am I taking advantage of God's grace and goodness, falsely assuming that His blessings are a sign that He has approved of my lifestyle?

Never   Much

1   2   3   4   5   6   7

Set a Goal

Using the seven-point evaluation scales, can you isolate one area in your life that needs the most attention? (Hint: Look for the high numbers!) As a result of this personal evaluation, what one goal would you like to set?

_____

_____

_____

_____

Memorize the Following Scripture

Therefore, I urge you, brothers, in view of God's mercy, to offer your bodies as living sacrifices, holy and pleasing to God—this is your spiritual act of worship. Do not conform any longer to the pattern of this world, but be transformed by the renewing of your mind. Then you will be able to test and approve what God's will is—his good, pleasing and perfect will.

ROMANS 12:1–2

Growing Together

The following questions are designed for small group discussion:

1. Can you share some current illustrations regarding how Christians today are living more "man-centered lives" than "God-centered lives"?

2. Without being judgmental, what direct teachings of Scripture can you cite that many Christians you know are choosing to disobey? What about your own life?

3. Again without being judgmental, can you cite some negative consequences you've witnessed because certain Christians have chosen to live out of the perfect will of God? What about negative consequences in your own life?

4. In what ways can we deceive ourselves into thinking God is approving our behavior when in reality He disapproves?

5. In what way can we pray for you specifically?

Chapter 11

A Second Chance

Read 1 Samuel 9:25–10:24

God is a "God of the second chance." This is one of the most positive and encouraging lessons we can learn from Israel's history. The Lord extended grace to His people again and again. When they repented and turned from their sins, God had mercy and compassion and restored them to a place of blessing and success.

In this chapter, however, we'll see God give the children of Israel a second chance even when they were still in a state of rebellion. They had not confessed their sins nor had they turned from their wicked ways. Yet, because of "his great name," and because He "was pleased to make" Israel "his own," He did "not reject his people" (1 Sam. 12:22). God had made an unconditional promise to Abraham and He would not violate who He is—the God of truth and righteousness (Gen. 12:1–3).

A Message from God

From what happened next, we can assume that Samuel did not tell Saul directly that evening on the rooftop that he was to be Israel's king (1 Sam. 9:25). If he did, Saul probably spent a sleepless night. We do know, however, that the next morning Saul received the full story. Before the sun came up, Samuel awakened Saul and his servant. After they had prepared themselves for the journey home, Samuel escorted

Saul to the edge of town and told him to send his servant on ahead so he could give the future king "a message from God" (9:27). At this moment, Samuel must have told Saul in no uncertain terms that God had chosen him to be the future king of Israel.

Three Affirming Signs

At this point in their conversation, Samuel "took a flask of oil and poured it on Saul's head and kissed, him saying, 'Has not the Lord anointed you leader over his inheritance?'" (1 Sam. 10:1).

God understood Saul's need for affirmation, just as He understood Moses' need centuries before when He called him to lead His people out of Egypt (Exod. 4:1–9). Consequently, God led Samuel to exercise his prophetic gift and tell Saul that He would experience three more miraculous signs to reassure him that his kingship was a divine appointment.

"Two Men at Rachel's Tomb"

The first prophecy related to Saul's personal concerns and anxiety regarding the lost donkeys. Saul first expressed these concerns to his servant before he had ever met Samuel. Next, when Saul first met Samuel, this old prophet had miraculously taken these very concerns and words out of Saul's heart and verbalized them back to Saul. And now as the two men were about to part, Samuel told Saul that on his journey home, he would meet two men who were total strangers— who would deliver the same basic message.

When this prophetic sign was fulfilled that very day (10:9), Saul could not deny that it was another supernatural demonstration to affirm his kingship. Samuel had read what was in his mind and now he had prophesied that two strangers would repeat back to him the same thoughts and concerns that were in his heart.

Saul's concerns (9:5)	Samuel's message when he first met Saul (9:20)	Samuel's prophecy regarding the two men (10:2)
"Come, let's go back, or my father will stop thinking about the donkeys and start worrying about us."	"As for donkeys you lost three days ago, do not worry about them; they have been found."	"They will say to you, 'The donkeys you set out to look for have been found. And now your father has stopped thinking about them and is worried about you. He is asking "What shall I do about my son?"'"

Figure 11.1

Note the clear details in this prophecy. Samuel would meet "two men." In terms of location, it would be "near Rachel's tomb." It would also happen in "Zelzah on the border of Benjamin." With these details, God wanted Saul to know beyond a shadow of a doubt that Samuel was "attested as a prophet of the Lord." Everything Samuel prophesied would come to pass. Not one word would "fall to the ground" unfulfilled (3:19–20).

Three Men Going up to God at Bethel

Again, note the detail in this next prophecy (10:3–4). Samuel told Saul than when he reached "the great tree at Tabor," he would meet "three men"—not "two" as before—men who were on their way to offer sacrifices at Bethel. They were headed for the very place God first appeared in a dream to Jacob—the father of all Israel. The first man would be carrying "three young goats"; the second would be carrying "three loaves of bread"; the third would be carrying "a skin of wine." When they saw Saul, they would greet him and offer him "two loaves of bread."

This prophecy also was fulfilled that very day, to the exact detail—another affirming sign that God, through Samuel, had called, appointed, and anointed Saul for this unique leadership role.

A Procession of Prophets

The third sign was the most dramatic (10:5–6). It would impact Saul's "heart"—his thoughts, his feelings, and his will. As he approached Gibeah—which was Saul's hometown—he would meet a large group of prophets—not two or three as before. They would all be prophesying, and Saul would be moved to join them. The words of Scripture speak clearly: "The Spirit of the LORD will come upon you in power, and you will prophesy with them; and you will be changed into a different person" (5:6).

Gibeah was a "Philistine outpost" (5:5). In other words, God chose to allow Saul to experience this dramatic miracle in the midst of the archenemies of Israel, demonstrating that He had chosen this young, impressive-looking man, not only to be king, but to lead His people into battle against the Philistines.

Again, every detail of this prophesy came to pass that very day (5:9–14). Having experienced these miraculous signs, Saul could not fail to understand God's intervention and involvement in his life.

A Changed Heart, a Different Person

What really happened to Saul when he met these prophets? While still with Samuel on the edge of town, "*God changed Saul's heart*" when he turned to leave Samuel (5:9).

Personally, I think Saul at that moment was "justified by faith." Like Abraham of old, it appears that Saul believed God's Word through Samuel and it "was credited to him as righteousness" (Rom. 4:22–23). Saul was "born-again" (John 3:3).

He had been circumcised as a "son of Jacob," but at this moment I believe God "circumcised his heart." In essence, this is what Paul was referring to in his letter to the Romans: "A man is not a Jew if he is only one outwardly, nor is circumcision merely outward and physical. No, a man is a Jew if he is one inwardly; and circumcision is circumcision of the heart, by the Spirit, not by the written code. Such a man's praise is not from men, but from God (Rom. 2:28–29).

When Saul joined the prophets, we also read that he was "*changed into a different person*" (1 Sam. 10:6). What began as a conversion experience—a heart change—on the edge of town became more complete, enabling Saul to act on these new thoughts and feelings.

Second Thoughts

Saul's heart and life were definitely changed. However, when we sense God's call in our lives, we still retain our same basic personalities. This was true of Saul. Though he knew that the Lord had called him to be king over all Israel, when he reached his hometown, he became very ambivalent and cautious. Samuel was not there to "hold his hand" and encourage him.

We see this hesitancy when Saul's uncle asked him what Samuel had said to him. He told him about the donkeys, but he did not tell his uncle what Samuel had said about the kingship" (10:16). He avoided discussing the very reason God had orchestrated his meeting with Samuel.

Did withholding this information reflect wisdom, discretion, and perhaps humility? Or was it anxiety, fear, and timidity? Personally, I believe Saul was having second thoughts. In spite of the undeniable miraculous signs and changes that had taken place in his life, Saul began to doubt—which is understandable. The magnitude of the challenge must have been overwhelming for a thirty-year-old farm boy from the tribe of

Benjamin. Under these circumstances, anyone might have second thoughts—no matter how much God had made His calling clear.

In Hiding

We can understand Saul's anxiety more easily when we "stand in his shoes" and listen to Samuel speak at Mizpah (10:17–19)—the very place the old prophet had stood years before and interceded for Israel prior to their victorious battle over the Philistines (7:5). Imagine how Saul felt when Samuel charged all Israel, reminding them of their rebellion: "'This is what the LORD, the God of Israel, says: "I brought Israel up out of Egypt, and I delivered you from the power of Egypt and all the kingdoms that oppressed you." But you have now rejected your God, who saves you out of all your calamities and distresses. And you have said, "No, set a king over us"'" (10:17–19).

No matter how much Samuel had prepared Saul for this moment, fear must have overwhelmed this young thirty-year-old. He knew that in spite of Israel's rebellious spirit, God was going to give them a "second chance" under his leadership. But the reality of it all hit Saul full force when he heard Samuel's reminder that all Israel had sinned in demanding a king. His humanness overshadowed God's affirmation in his life.

The tension in Saul's heart also intensified greatly as he watched the leaders in Israel cast lots to determine who this king would be (10:20–21). Of course, he already knew. He had already been anointed. But to see the selection process gradually unfolding before his eyes must have been terribly unnerving! First, his tribe "was chosen"; second, his clan "was chosen"; and finally, Saul "was chosen."

At some point, Saul couldn't handle the anxiety that was building up within him. In spite of his "changed heart" and God's affirmations, he could not face this awesome responsibility. He ran away and hid "himself among the baggage" (10:22).

Long Live the King

Imagine the scene. God's one and only candidate for king is hiding in the midst of boxes, blankets, baskets, and all of the other things the children of Israel brought with them as they responded to Samuel's call to come to Mizpah. The stage was set, the curtain had been raised, but Saul couldn't walk on stage. Those in charge who were functioning under Samuel's direction, "inquired further of the Lord," and God responded, specifying exactly where Saul was hiding. If God could find lost donkeys and tell others where they were hiding, He could certainly do the same thing with the future king of Israel.

When the delegation found Saul, he must have turned beet-red. He had to be embarrassed, even though he would probably have been relieved if he had been rejected for his cowardice. But the leaders in Israel were not going to be denied. Everyone was convinced he was God's choice. They brought Saul out and there he stood—"a head taller than any of the others!" (10:23). When Samuel presented him to the people, they were impressed—and elated. They shouted, "Long live the king!" (10:24).

Becoming God's Man Today

Principles to Live By

Of all the lessons that we can learn from this study of Samuel's life, the following principles are most encouraging. They focus on God's grace and love for all of us who are His children—even when we walk out of His will.

Principle 1. God is willing and waiting to give all of His children a second chance.

God is a God of the second chance. This is the "lead line" in this chapter, which is very reassuring. For Israel, the second chance often came with a whole new generation. But when Saul was anointed as king, God gave Israel another chance immediately. After briefly reviewing Israel's history and pointing out how God had responded to their cries for help on previous occasions, Samuel charged all Israel and their new king to remain loyal to the Lord: "If you fear the LORD and serve and obey him," Samuel warned, "and do not rebel against his command, and if both you and the king who reigns over you follow the LORD your God—good!" (12:14).

"His Good, Pleasing and Perfect Will"

According to the Apostle Paul, God's perfect will is good (Rom. 12:2). The Lord was willing to forgive the children of Israel for their selfish decision in demanding a king. He was willing to bless them in spite of their hard-heartedness. He was even willing to overlook their sin when they wanted to replace the King of Kings with Saul. His only condition was that they repent and walk in His will.

Today, God will also give His children second chances. The most wonderful truth in all of Scripture is that the blood of Jesus Christ keeps on cleansing us from our sins. John wrote that "if we confess our sins, he is faithful and just and will forgive us our sins and purify us from all unrighteousness" (1 John 1:9).

This does not mean that we will not be disciplined when we rebel against the Lord. Rather, it means that God always gives repentant Christians another chance to please Him and to experience the fullness of His blessings.

God's Wonderful Grace

As I was teaching Samuel's life to the believers I minister to each Sunday at Fellowship Bible Church North, I also had the privilege of participating in our annual church ski trip in the Colorado Rockies. Each evening I conducted a Bible study and time of sharing. One evening I asked everyone to discuss the "second chance" principle and to share how they had experienced God's second chances, either in their own lives or in the lives of people they knew. I'll never forget the response of one person who said, "I've not only experienced God's second chance, but His third, fourth, fifth, etc., chances in my life." In essence, he was talking about God's wonderful grace and forgiveness.

At times when I'm personally struggling to make decisions that are in God's will and at times when I fail, I've asked the Lord not only for His help to make the right decision but to be patient with me when I've made the wrong decisions. I've asked for time to make mid-course corrections. I'm thankful for His grace and forgiveness—which I never want to abuse—but, to be perfectly honest, it's easy to do!

Do you believe God will give you another chance to return to His perfect will. I know He will. He did it for Israel again and again, and He will certainly do it for you—and me!

Principle 2. God normally brings others into our lives to enable us to have a second chances—even when it is difficult or impossible to explain.

In this study, the person was Saul. And what makes this event so unique is that the person God chose was to occupy the position God had both approved and also had rejected. He had approved the position centuries before but the way the elders of Israel proceeded definitely led them out of God's perfect will.

Joseph's Divine Perspective

God did virtually the same thing when He used Joseph to deliver his father's family from starvation by bringing them all to Egypt. His brothers committed a very evil deed when they sold Joseph into Egyptian slavery. But God used it to save their lives.

We cannot even begin to explain satisfactorily Joseph's divine perspective, but it's true nevertheless: "But Joseph said to them, 'Don't be afraid. Am I in the place of God? You intended to harm me, but God intended it for good to accomplish what is now being done, the saving of many lives'" (Gen. 50:19–20).[1]

David's Grace Experience

David is another illustration. When this man after God's own heart sinned so terribly against God by committing adultery and murder, God sent the prophet Nathan to rescue him from his blindness. Though David suffered the consequences of his sin the rest of his life, he repented and experienced God's forgiveness. God gave David a second chance, even though, according to the Law he should have died because of his sin.[2]

The truth is that we've all been given a second chance if we know Jesus Christ as personal Savior. Ironically, God later chose another man whose name was Saul—this time a persecutor of the church. God also changed this man's heart and life and then charged him to carry the gospel to the Gentiles. God used the apostle Paul to tell all of us about a second chance.

"Carry Each Other's Burdens"

God also uses other Christians to help those of us who get trapped in sin. Consider Paul's words to the Galatians: "Brothers, if someone is caught in a sin, you who are spiritual should restore him gently. But watch yourself, or you also may be tempted. Carry each other's burdens, and in this way you will fulfill the law of Christ" (Gal. 6:1–2).

If you're really out of God's will, don't be surprised if God uses other believers—Christians who are sensitive to God's Holy Spirit—to say something or do something that will set off a warning signal in your life. When this happens, don't turn a deaf ear, but see it as God's way of giving you a second chance.

Principle 3. If God calls us to help someone to have a second chance, He will encourage and enable us to face the challenge, even though we may feel inadequate.

King Saul's challenge was awesome. It's no wonder he ran and hid "among the baggage." But God knew how tough this divine assignment would be. Consequently, He used Samuel to reassure Saul he could do the job. Think of the affirmations through this old prophet:

- He enabled Samuel to know Saul's mind and reveal that his donkeys had been found.
- He had Samuel prepare a special meal for Saul before he ever met this man.
- He caused Samuel to prophesy accurately that he would receive three more signs to affirm God's calling to be king (and all came to pass in every detail).

God knew how frightened and intimidated Saul would be. Consequently, He worked miracle after miracle to assure Saul that He was on his side and would enable him to carry out his task.

The Power of God's Presence

Most importantly, God changed Saul's heart and filled him with the Holy Spirit—something God will do for all of us when we turn our lives over to Him. Though Saul's experience was certainly unique, the Bible says that if we're "in Christ," we're new creations—we're born again (2 Cor. 5:17; John 3:3). This, of course, is the greatest second chance we'll ever experience!

Paul's Words of Encouragement

The apostle Paul, who experienced unusual persecution, testified and verified that he could do all things through Christ's strength (Phil. 4:13). Furthermore, he assured the Philippians with this wonderful promise: "And my God will meet all your needs according to his glorious riches in Christ Jesus" (4:19).

Paul also gave this reassuring testimony when he wrote to the Corinthians: "We are hard pressed on every side, but not crushed; perplexed, but not in despair; persecuted, but not abandoned; struck down, but not destroyed. . . . . All this is for your benefit, so that the grace that is reaching more and more people may cause thanksgiving to overflow to the glory of God. Therefore we do not lose heart. Though outwardly we are wasting away, yet inwardly we are being renewed day by day" (2 Cor. 4:8–9; 15–16).

Principle 4. Our opportunity for a second chance ceases when we come to the end of our lives.

The author of Hebrews wrote these rather chilling words: "Just as man is destined to die once, and after that to face judgment" (9:27).

God's Word is clear: There are no second chances after death.

When Adam and Eve sinned, they plunged the whole world into sin. And when Paul wrote to the Romans, he made it very clear that "the wages of sin is death" (6:23). It's obvious, both theologically and experientially, that we all need a savior from our sins. God wants us to have a second chance— a chance to be saved.

Don't miss God's "second chance"! Receive the Lord Jesus Christ as personal Savior. "Today, if you hear his voice, do not harden your hearts" (Heb. 3:7).

Personalizing These Principles

Read the following questions carefully and prayerfully. Ask the Holy Spirit to enable you to respond to His Word.

1. Have you committed a sin against God that you feel is unpardonable?

The Bible has good news! No matter what your sin, great or small, you can experience the forgiveness of the Lord Jesus Christ and be restored to fellowship with Him and once again walk in His perfect will. Again, remember the wonderful promise in John's epistle: "If we confess our sins, he is faithful and just and will forgive us our sins and purify us from all unrighteousness" (1 John 1:9).

2. Are you too prideful to admit that you need someone else to assist you in being restored to fellowship with God?

All of us need others in our lives. This is the uniqueness within the body of Jesus Christ. This is why we all need each other. No member of the body can say that he doesn't need another member. Paul made it clear that we are to "teach and admonish one another" (Col. 3:16). Listen also to the words of James: "Therefore confess your sins to each other and pray for each other so that you may be healed" (James 5:16).

3. Do you feel intimidated and inadequate to help someone else who needs to be directed back into God's perfect will?

This is true of most of us. But when we are weak, God can make us strong. Remember Paul's words to Timothy when he felt intimidated: "For God did not give us a spirit of timidity, but a spirit of power, of love and of self-discipline" (2 Tim. 1:7).

4. Are you a born-again Christian, or do you still need a savior from your sins?

Many people believe in Jesus Christ—that He lived and died, and even rose again. But have you received the Lord Jesus Christ as your own personal Savior?

If you're not sure, respond to the wonderful promise that John gave us in his gospel: "He came to that which was his own [the nation of Israel], but his own did not receive him. Yet to all who received him [both Jew and Gentile], to those who believed in his name, he gave the right to become children of God—children born not of natural descent, nor of human decision or a husband's will, but born of God" (John 1:11–13).

Set a Goal

As a result of this personal evaluation, what has the Holy Spirit revealed to you? Write out one goal that you need to set for your life:

_____

_____

_____

_____

Memorize the Following Scripture

But do not forget this one thing, dear friends: With the Lord a day is like a thousand years, and a thousand years are like a day. The Lord is not slow in keeping his promise, as some understand slowness. He is patient with you, not wanting anyone to perish, but everyone to come to repentance.
2 PETER 3:8–9

Growing Together

The following questions are designed for small group discussion:

1. What second chances have you experienced in your own life? What second chances have you seen others experience?

2. Would you share with us a person (or persons) that God has brought into your life to give you a second chance?

3. How have you experienced God's encouragement and enablement to help you help someone else have a second chance?

4. Would you share your personal testimony regarding how you came to know the Lord Jesus Christ as your personal Savior?

5. In what way can we pray for you specifically?

Chapter 12

A Man of Character
Read 1 Samuel 12:1–25

As you reflect on Christian men you've known during your lifetime—particularly those who are up in years—how many can you name who have consistently walked with God from childhood? In some respects, this is an unfair question since many of us have not had the privilege of knowing too many men for a lifetime.

A Man Who Marked My Life

The first man I thought of is my own dad. He was over thirty years old when I was born. I really have very little information about the first three decades of his life. I only know that from the time I began to know him, I remember a man who worked very hard at being a consistent Christian.

In terms of specific character traits, I never saw him lie or cheat. He was a gentle, caring person. He was incredibly loyal to my mom and to all of his children. He got up at four o'clock every morning to milk the cows and worked hard all day to make a living for the family. In terms of spiritual leadership, he was also deeply concerned about people who didn't know the Lord Jesus Christ as their personal Savior. Though he tended to be very passive in confronting problems, I never saw him purposely hurt or mistreat anyone. In fact, he also went the extra mile to be a peacemaker. Needless to say, from the time I came to know my father, his life marked my own.

In spite of a sixth-grade education, Dad loved the Lord and taught me to do the same.

God's Limited Few

Even in Scripture we have limited examples of men who lived a lifetime devoted to the Lord. This is why Samuel stands out in Scripture as an unusual man of character. Though there are some large gaps in what we know about his years on this earth, we're told enough to conclude that he practiced what he preached most of his life.

We don't know how long Samuel lived after Saul became the leader in Israel, but we do know that he was "old and gray" when he anointed Saul as king (1 Sam. 12:2). To this point in his life, Samuel had served God and all Israel from the time he was just a small boy. As we read what is recorded from his farewell speech (1 Sam. 12), we can learn a great deal about his love for God and his integrity among his fellow Israelites.

"I Have Listened"

After Saul led an army of three hundred thirty-three thousand to a great victory over the Ammonites (11:1–11), Samuel assembled the children of Israel at Gilgal (11:14). There he "reaffirmed" Saul as king and led the people in a great celebration as they "sacrificed fellowship offerings before the LORD" (11:15). He then delivered a passionate speech that demonstrated the kind of man he really was.

Samuel's opening line testifies to his obedience to God. "Samuel said to all Israel, 'I have listened to everything you said to me and have set a king over you'" (12:1).

Samuel was referring to both Israel's demand and God's approval—with a focus on God's approval. Earlier the Lord had said—'Listen to them and give them a king'" (8:22a). Though Samuel knew Israel's demand was selfish and out of the perfect will of God, he also knew the Lord was going to grant their request. In spite of his own reluctance, Samuel religiously followed God's instructions. This was the story of his life. As a young boy, he had learned this lesson from Eli, the high priest, even though he had had to deliver a very difficult message to this old man (3:17–21).

From that point forward, whenever God spoke directly to Samuel and gave him a message to deliver to all Israel or to someone specifically, he served the Lord's people as a faithful prophet and judge. And now he was "old and gray." In his farewell speech he reminded Israel that he had been their "leader" from his "youth until this day" (12:2b).

"Here I Stand"

What a scene it must have been! In his humanness, Samuel was still hurting emotionally, even though he knew he had obeyed God by anointing Saul as king. The leaders in Israel had rejected God (8:7), but Samuel still felt the pain himself. To this point, he had been their faithful leader. He had always delivered God's message to Israel. He had been the instrument God had used to set them free from Philistine bondage. In fact, "throughout Samuel's lifetime, the hand of the LORD was against the Philistines" (7:13b).

It's understandable that Samuel would still feel the hurt that always accompanies rejection. Even though he knew in his head that he was not the ultimate target of Israel's rebellion, he still felt the pain in his heart. At this moment, his relationship with God was so intimate that he could not detach himself psychologically and spiritually from what had happened. To "reject God" was to "reject him."

A Lesson in Vulnerability

Samuel defended his character publicly. Perhaps he needed the reassurance that he had not failed to be a good leader. Demonstrating unusual vulnerability, he laid his heart open before everyone. With a series of questions, he asked God's people to "testify against" him "in the presence of the LORD" and in the presence of the newly anointed king (12:3):

- Whose ox have I taken?
- Whose donkey have I taken?
- Whom have I cheated?
- Whom have I oppressed?
- From whose hand have I accepted a bribe to make me shut my eyes?

An Example of Sincerity

With obvious sincerity, Samuel concluded this series of questions with a statement that would once and for all clear his name from any criticisms: "'If I have done any of these, I will make it right.'"

Israel's response to Samuel's questions must have been incredibly reassuring to this old prophet and judge. "'You have not cheated or oppressed us,' they replied. 'You have not taken anything from anyone's hands'" (12:4).

When Samuel heard this positive response, he reminded the people that God was listening—and so was Saul: "Samuel said to them, 'The LORD is witness against you, and also his anointed is witness this day, that you have not found anything in my hand.' 'He is witness,' they said" (12:5).

"Now Then, Stand Here"

After Samuel cleared his own reputation with the children of Israel, he felt free in his spirit to challenge and exhort them regarding their sins against God. "Here I stand," he said, offering to correct anything he had done wrong. And once the leaders in Israel had verified his character, he challenged them to "trade places" with him. "'Now, then, stand here!'" he charged (2:7). It was their time to check their own character. After all,

Samuel had been vulnerable and sincere. Now he asked the children of Israel to do the same. Obviously, he had earned the right—not just with words but with a lifetime of demonstrating his integrity and commitment to doing the will of God.

God's Faithfulness

In essence, Samuel wanted all Israel to know that God had taken care of them for centuries without appointing a king to lead them. The LORD had called the prophet Moses and his brother Aaron to be their deliverers. With God's help and a manifestation of His mighty power, these two men had led Israel out of Egypt and into the Promised Land (2:6–7). He first enabled Moses and Aaron to bring the awesome and horrible plagues on Egypt. He charged Moses to stretch out his hand and part the Red Sea. And once in the wilderness, God supplied them with manna and water.

Disobedience and Defeat

Samuel reminded this present generation of Israelites that in spite of God's faithfulness, their forefathers had forgotten "the LORD their God" (2:9). The result was defeat and bondage. Illustrating what happened, Samuel also reminded them that the Lord had "sold them into the hands of Sisera" (Judg. 4:2–3) and into the hands of "the Philistines and the king of Moab" (Judg. 3:12–14; 10:6–8).

Repentance and Restoration

Most importantly, Samuel reminded Israel of God's compassion and grace. Each time they got into serious trouble because of their disobedience, God responded to their repentance and cries for help. He sent leaders such as Jerub-Baal (Gideon), Barak, and Jephthah. Samuel also reminded them that he had been their most recent leader. Each time God had used these leaders, and a number of others, to deliver His people from their enemies (1 Sam. 12:10–11).

"Now Here Is the King"

With this historical review, Samuel was laying the foundation for making a very important point. Though God had been their divine and faithful King throughout the centuries, they had now rejected God and had asked for a human king (12:12). They deliberately rejected the Lord, forgetting that He had always had compassion on his people when they turned from their idolatry and sin. No doubt gesturing to Saul, he proclaimed for all to hear: "Now here is the king you have chosen, the one you asked for; see, the LORD has set a king over you" (12:13).

A True Pastoral Heart

By this time, the children of Israel must have been getting very nervous and tense. Samuel had put his finger on their sinful attitudes and actions. They couldn't miss this message. At this point he could have used his own feelings of hurt and rejection to "twist the knife" he had already inserted into their consciences in order to get their attention. Instead he quickly reassured them that God would still bless them in spite of their self-centered and carnal behavior: "If you fear the LORD and serve and obey him and do not rebel against his commands, and if both you and the king who reigns over you follow the LORD your God—good!" (12:14).

With this message of hope, however, Samuel also added a serious warning—one that had been issued to Israel many times before: "But if you do not obey the LORD, and if you rebel against his commands, his hand will be against you, as it was against your fathers" (12:15).

"Now Then, Stand Still"

Early on in this speech, Samuel had issued a charge for all Israel to "stand" in front of him (12:7). He wanted their undivided attention. He wanted them to hear every word he was about to utter. But now he asked them to "stand still"—not to hear from him but to witness another great miracle.

It was not accidental that Samuel's charge at this moment in Israel's history is almost identical to Moses' charge as the children of Israel stood on the edge of the Red Sea. Pharaoh and his army were converging on this unarmed group of men, women, and children. At that moment, Moses prophesied and cried out, "Stand still and see the salvation of the LORD" (Exod. 14:13 NKJ).

A Sigh of Relief

Following Samuel's words that God would still bless them in spite of their demand for a king, the children of Israel must have breathed a sigh of relief, perhaps taking their sinful actions lightly. But with another touch of grace and mercy, God used Samuel to send all Israel a serious warning that went far beyond Samuel's verbal exhortations—a warning that spelled out a very clear message that God never takes sin lightly even though He had promised to bless them in spite of their sin.

A Lesson from History

To demonstrate that God was still God and that He was still their sovereign king in spite of their rejection, Samuel unveiled a great miracle. He took them back in time—back to Egypt, back to the wilderness, back to the dramatic scene when their forefathers had crossed the Red Sea and later over Jordan. Samuel wanted all Israel—not just the leaders—to understand clearly that they had done a very "evil thing . . . in the eyes of the LORD when" they had "asked for a king" (1 Sam. 12:17). To get this point across in no uncertain terms, he prayed and asked God to send "thunder and rain" during the time they were harvesting wheat (12:17–18).

It never rained at this time of the year in the land of Canaan. This was a miracle, a definite act of God that overruled the normal course of nature. The children of Israel knew this very well and they "stood in awe of the LORD and of Samuel."

A Moment of Glory

Isn't it interesting that at this moment, Samuel was back in the limelight in Israel's thoughts and feelings. They not only stood in awe of the Lord but also of Samuel. In this sense, God was defending His servant and allowing him to share in His glory—something God did with very few men He chose to lead Israel.

Moses was one of those men. In the midst of demonstrating to Israel that He was still the sovereign king, the Lord was sensitive to Samuel's feelings of rejection and hurt. By allowing him to be a human instrument in working this great miracle, God was restoring Samuel's self-confidence and rebuilding his self-image, as He had done for Moses.[1]

Something to Remember

Reassuring Samuel was certainly important but only a secondary result of the miracle. The primary reason God sent the devastating storm during the dry season—which no doubt wiped out their wheat harvest—was to get Israel's attention and to reinforce the seriousness of their sin. Predictably, it worked: "The people all said to Samuel, 'Pray to the LORD your God for your servants so that we will not die, for we have added to all our other sins the evil of asking for a king'" (12:19).

"Do Not Be Afraid"

At this moment, God's people didn't turn to their newly appointed king, they turned to Samuel. From a human point of view this must have been a very rewarding experience for this old man who had faithfully served as their leader but whom they had set aside for selfish and sinful reasons.

At this moment we also get another glimpse into Samuel's sterling character. A lesser man would have used this incredible platform to take control, to parade his own sense of self-importance, and to attempt to regain his position in Israel. How easily he could have rationalized all of these motives and intentions, especially since Israel had sinned against the Lord by asking for a king.

Seizing the Moment for God

Though Samuel may have been tempted to seize the moment for his own advantage, he immediately demonstrated his pastoral heart. He calmed their fears and reassured them that even though they had sinned, the Lord would not forsake them. Even though they had been faithless, God would be faithful in carrying out His covenant with Abraham, Isaac, and Jacob (12:22).

Rather than using what happened as a platform to bolster his public image in the political arena, Samuel demonstrated his loyalty to these people by exhorting them to "serve the Lord" with all their hearts (12:20). More specifically, Samuel warned: "Do not turn away after useless idols. They can do you no good, nor can they rescue you, because they are useless" (12:21).

Speaking the Truth in Love

In the final words of his farewell speech Samuel did not allow his hurt feelings and resentments to cause him to retaliate and get even, on the one hand, or to forsake Israel, withdraw, and "lick his wounds," on the other. Note the incredible compassion blended with a commitment to always "speak the truth in love": "'As for me, far be it from me that I should sin against the Lord by failing to pray for you. And I will teach you the way that is good and right. But be sure to fear the Lord and serve him faithfully with all your heart; consider what great things he has done for you. Yet if you persist in doing evil, both you and your king will be swept away'" (12:23–25).

Becoming God's Man Today

Principles to Live By

The principles that come down to each one of us through Samuel's sterling character are powerful and penetrating. They're very encouraging as well as convicting!

Principle 1. No matter what our past failures, God still wants us to be men and women who reflect His character.

Samuel wasn't perfect. He certainly made mistakes like all of us. But like Timothy, he had the unique privilege of learning the Holy Scriptures "from infancy." For Timothy, this spiritual foundation made him "wise for salvation through faith in Christ Jesus" (2 Tim. 3:15) and eventually helped him develop into a "man of God" (3:17). Though Samuel looked forward to the cross and Timothy looked back to the cross, they were both justified by faith—just like the patriarch, Abraham, in the Old Testament and the apostle Paul in the New Testament.

The facts are that Samuel and Timothy and a few others like Joshua, Joseph, and Daniel are rather rare examples in Scripture. They followed God faithfully early in life. Many men who eventually became examples did so later in life.

So it is today. Most of us are like the majority in Israel. We've disobeyed God and walked out of His will. We've resisted the Holy Spirit. Eventually, however, we put our faith in Jesus Christ for salvation and began to experience the abundant life that God destined for us. Like many in Israel, we can begin where we are—at any given moment in our lives—to develop godly character. We can forget "what is behind" and "press on towards the goal to win the prize for which God has called 'us' heavenward in Christ Jesus" (Phil. 3:13–14).

Furthermore, it's wonderful to know that even as Christians, when we disobey and wander out of His will, we are always welcome back into the fold. Like the father who welcomed the prodigal son back home again after he spent his fortune in riotous living, God the Father will always welcome His children "back home again."

Principle 2. We can only build godly character through obedience to God's will as revealed in the Holy Scriptures and by the power of the Holy Spirit.

To develop godly character, the first step we must take is to receive the Lord Jesus Christ as our personal Savior. Paul made this clear in his letter to the Ephesians when he wrote: "For it is by grace you have been saved, through faith—and this not from yourselves, it is the gift of God—not by works, so that no one can boast" (Eph. 3:8–9).

The Maximum Man

No man has ever earned his way to heaven. Salvation is a gift of God. It is received through faith and faith alone. In fact, we cannot even receive Jesus Christ apart from the ministry of the Holy Spirit who convicts us of sin and then places us in the body of Christ when we're born again (John 3:3–8; 1 Cor. 12:13).

However, once we become Christians, we are to develop godly character that reflects the maximum man, Jesus Christ. As Paul wrote to the Philippians, our "attitude should be the same as Christ Jesus" (Phil. 2:5). We are to imitate the Savior and follow His example (1 Cor. 11:1).

We Are "God's Workmanship"

Paul also underscored this truth in his letter to the Ephesians after he made it clear that we're saved by grace through faith and not by works (Eph. 2:8–9). Once we become new creations in Christ (2 Cor. 5:17), we have become "God's workmanship, created in Christ Jesus *to do good works,* which God prepared in advance for us to do" (Eph. 2:10, emphasis mine).

God in His grace has also made it possible for us to develop this godly character through the indwelling presence of the Holy Spirit. As we yield our lives to God, He transforms us into His image, enabling us to reflect the fruit of the Spirit, which "is love, joy, peace, patience, kindness, goodness, faithfulness, gentleness and self-control" (Gal. 5:22–23).

Godly Character Is Not Automatic

This does not mean we will automatically develop godly character as Christians. Though it's God's will that we become more and more like His Son, we can choose to disobey and walk out of His will. Like the Corinthians, we can decide to be carnal and fleshly (1 Cor. 3:3). Though God will discipline us if we're true sons (Heb. 12:8), we can still wallow in sin and suffer the consequences.

Don't misunderstand. We're all tempted to make decisions that are out of the will of God. Even Jesus Christ in His human nature was tempted to sin just as we are tempted, but, of course, He "was without sin" because of His divine nature. That's why He can be our perfect Savior and High Priest (Heb. 4:14–16). But thank God, when we are tempted to sin, "He will also provide a way out"—if we're willing to take the escape route (1 Cor. 10:13).

A Real Life Experience

I had an interesting temptation to violate godly character the week I was working on this chapter. I leased a car in Denver and drove to Beaver Creek, Colorado. On the way, we stopped to eat. Backing into a parking place, I rammed into the bumper of a pickup truck and made a sizable dent in my trunk. I discovered that I could restore it somewhat with some well-placed taps from the inside. However, one could still see the damage.

For several days I struggled with whether or not I should report this damage when I returned the car. I'd been down this road before—turning in cars. I knew the "rules." I knew rental companies didn't check that carefully, especially if the car is filthy from dirt and grime that accumulates from the roads in Colorado. And once the paperwork was done, I also knew they would have no proof that they had not missed the dent on a previous rental.

Finally, after several days, I knew what I must do to keep a clear conscience. I reported it, which surprised the attendant at the counter. As I predicted, no one even checked the car. I filled out a form on the damage and then couldn't help but notice the expression that came on the attendant's face when she read where I was employed.

"Are you a pastor?" she asked, as she looked up at me with a smile on her face. "Yes, I am!" I said proudly.

Isn't it amazing how good we feel when we do what is right? Little did she realize how close I came to violating what Paul meant when he said a person with godly character should be "above reproach" in matters such as this. Yes, I was tempted—but God provided a way of escape! I simply needed to tell the truth.

Samuel is a great example. He beautifully illustrates obedience to God. He made choices that were in harmony with the will of God. Though he was certainly tempted to violate God's standards, most of his choices certainly reflected the God he served.

Principle 3. Godly character gives us the credibility and right to help others develop the same qualities.

Before Samuel exhorted the children of Israel regarding their sin against God, he subjected himself to careful scrutiny and evaluation. He asked a series of very pointed questions, to which all Israel responded positively. He had practiced what he had preached all of his life! He earned the right to exhort his fellow Israelites regarding their sins.

This does not mean we have to live perfect Christian lives to be effective as fathers, mothers, pastors, and teachers. That is humanly impossible. However, it does mean we should live at a level of consistency that is noted and respected. And when we make mistakes and fail God and others, it means acknowledging these mistakes and seeking forgiveness. This in itself helps us develop credibility and makes us able to teach and admonish others effectively.

Principle 4. God will never forsake us even though others may reject our efforts of loving concern and exhortation.

I love the way God was sensitive to Samuel's feelings of rejection, which certainly resulted in feelings of failure. If we love God and we serve Him faithfully, even though people may reject God's Word which we're teaching, it's difficult to separate our personal identity from the Lord.

As a pastor, I certainly struggle with these feelings. I know in my head that when people reject the Word of God which I'm teaching, they're not really rejecting me but God. Yet they *are* rejecting me since I am God's representative. There's no way to escape those feelings of hurt.

Don't misunderstand. There are times when I have said things or done things in ways that bring personal rejection. In these situations, people reject the truth—and me—because I've been harsh or insensitive. I've violated biblical principles of communication. In those cases, I've deserved rejection. But even when we "speak the truth in love"—like I believe Samuel did—we will still feel rejection.

This past year, I received at least two letters from people that devastated me. They had nothing good to say about me or my ministry. They filled paragraph after paragraph with angry and vitriolic accusations. As I do in these instances, I asked the Lord for encouragement and insight. I also took these letters to the team of people who work with me day after day—those who really know me—and asked for their evaluation. I was greatly encouraged when they all informed me that these accusations were false and a reflection of the hearts of those that wrote the letters. Not that I don't make mistakes. All who know me know I do, but they reassured me "they didn't know the person described in these letters." What a relief!

It's at times like these that God desires to build us up and provide opportunities that bring positive feedback. Again and again I've seen this happen, particularly when I've asked God for comfort and encouragement.

Remember, too, that when people are convicted by the Word of God and do not respond positively, they usually don't attack God. That's the ultimate in arrogance. However, they often rationalize and attack God's mouthpiece. This happened time and again to those godly prophets in Israel. We shouldn't be surprised when it happens to us.

Principle 5. If we are men of character, we will always demonstrate love and concern for others no matter how much they reject us and the truth.

This is probably one of the most challenging principles that emerges from the study of Samuel's life. Even though all Israel deserved to be left to fend for themselves and to wallow in the mess they had created, Samuel "turned the other cheek." Even though he was probably tempted to use this opportunity for political advantage and to retaliate, he encouraged the people not to be afraid. Perhaps his strongest and most convicting statement is as follows: "As for me, far be it from me that I should sin against the LORD by failing to pray for you. And I will teach you the way that is good and right" (1 Sam. 12:23).

When Jesus delivered His marvelous and powerful Sermon on the Mount, He said: "'You have heard that it was said, "Love your neighbor and hate your enemy." But I tell you: Love your enemies and pray for those who persecute you, that you may be sons of your Father in heaven'" (Matt. 5:43–45a). Is this possible? Yes, with God's help, we can develop godly character.

Personalizing These Principles

The following questions are designed to help you apply these principles in your life, which in turn, will help you develop godly character:

1. Where are you in your character-building experience? How would you measure yourself against the "maximum man" Jesus Christ?

   Don't be too hard on yourself. Remember that God evaluates our lives by how far we've come in the light of our opportunities for growth, not by how far we're behind because of our ignorance.

2. How aware are you of God's standard for godly character? To what extent do you understand the power of the indwelling Spirit and the fruit He desires to manifest through your life?

   For a dynamic study regarding God's standard for measuring Christian character, see *The Measure of a Man,* Gene A. Getz, (Regal Books, 1995). This study is based on Paul's letters to Timothy and Titus.

3. To what extent do you feel you are qualified to exhort others regarding godly character?

   You don't have to be perfect to help others mature in Christ. What's important is honesty that reflects where you are in your own spiritual journey and your plan for reflecting more and more of Christ's character.

4. How often do you feel rejected by others when they reject your efforts at communicating Christ's character?

Remember that it's normal to feel this rejection, particularly if you have a close relationship with Jesus Christ. Timothy felt this rejection and needed to be encouraged by Paul who wrote: "For God did not give us a spirit of timidity, but a spirit of power, of love and of self-discipline" (2 Tim. 1:7).

5. To what extent do you have difficulty forgiving others and praying for those who reject your efforts at communicating both by example and words that it is God's will for all people to live a godly life?

Remember that forgiveness is an act of the will in spite of how we feel. Negative feelings do not mean we haven't forgiven others. However, true forgiveness keeps negative feelings from causing us to be bitter and vindictive.

Set a Goal

As you've reflected on these questions and comments, what area has the Holy Spirit surfaced that needs special attention? Set at least one goal for your life:

_____

_____

_____

_____

Memorize the Following Scripture

But the fruit of the Spirit is love, joy, peace, patience, kindness, goodness, faithfulness, gentleness and self-control. Against such things there is no law.

GALATIANS 5:22–23

Growing Together

The following questions are designed for small group discussion.

1. When did you become a Christian and begin to develop character traits that reflect the "maximum man" Jesus Christ?

2. If you have a specific plan for developing godly character in your life, would you mind sharing that plan with the rest of us?

3. What examples can you share where godly character has given someone credibility for communicating God's standard of righteousness to others? Can you give us some examples, without being critical, in which you have seen the opposite take place? Feel free to give personal illustrations as well.

4. How has God encouraged you when you have been rejected by people who are in essence rejecting the God you serve?

5. If you are having a personal struggle forgiving someone and praying for that person, would you mind sharing your experience so we can pray for you?

Chapter 13

A Final Painful Task
Read 1 Samuel 13:1–14; 15:1–16:7

One of the most painful experiences I've ever faced is confronting a fellow Christian after years of friendship and fellowship in Jesus Christ. What has made this particularly agonizing is that it has led to a broken relationship that has never been healed and restored. Just recently I heard of one such person who still deeply resents my interfering with an adulterous relationship that devastated a number of people who looked to this individual as a role model. When I heard this report, I was deeply saddened since I still love this person deeply and always will.

This happened to Samuel in his relationship with King Saul. If he was to obey God and do what was best for all Israel, he had no choice but to confront sin in this man's life.

It was a painful experience for this old man—especially after he had reassured Saul that if he walked in God's will, all would go well with him and the people he led. Sadly, Saul did not respond positively to Samuel's exhortations. He allowed bitterness to wither his soul and destroy his life.

A Tragic Story

The story of Saul's kingship is one of the most tragic in the Bible. He had every opportunity to succeed, in spite of Israel's sin in asking for a king. However, pride became Saul's downfall.

The sin that led the Lord to ultimately reject Saul as king involved the Amelekites, who were very wicked people (Exod. 17:8–16).

Moses had reminded the children of Israel before they ever entered the land of Canaan that these people "had no fear of God" whatsoever (Deut. 25:18). In spite of God's terrible plagues on Egypt and in spite of the powerful miracle when God saved Israel from the Egyptians by parting the Red Sea, Amalek led his army against God's defenseless people. As Moses stated, when they "were weary and worn out," the Amalekites met them and "cut off all who were lagging behind."

Because of this terrible deed, God's hand of judgment fell on the Amalekites. They were unrepentant, even though God gave Joshua, Moses' military commander, victory over them (Exod. 17:13). At that time, God had said, "'I will completely blot out the memory of Amalek from under heaven'" (17:14). Like their other pagan neighbors, they continued to worship idols and engaged in horrible idolatry and immorality, at times even offering their own children as human sacrifices. Their behavior was a stench in the nostrils of God.

When Saul became king, the Lord commanded Saul through Samuel to bring judgement on those people. It was a specific message: "'"I will punish the Amalekites for what they did to Israel when they waylaid them as they came up from Egypt. Now go, attack the Amalekites and totally destroy everything that belongs to them. Do not spare them; put to death men and women, children and infants, cattle and sheep, camels and donkeys"'" (1 Sam. 15:2–3).

Partial Obedience

Saul took God's message through Samuel to heart—at least part of it! He "attacked the Amalekites all the way from Havilah to Shur, to the east of Egypt" (1 Sam. 15:7). But Saul did not obey God completely. He captured "Agag king of the Amalekites alive"—a direct violation of God's command (15:8a). Furthermore, he kept "the best of the sheep and cattle, the fat calves and lambs—everything that was good." On the other hand, "everything that was despised and weak," Saul and his army "totally destroyed" (15:9).

This was deliberate disobedience! Saul had heard everything that God had said. Why he took Agag alive remains open to speculation. Perhaps he was demonstrating his own superiority and military prowess by comparing himself with a king he had taken into bondage. Considering his attempt to prove himself at this moment in his life, this conclusion makes sense.

A Troubling Message

When Saul violated God's will, the Lord once again spoke to Samuel. The message was direct and to the point. "'I am grieved that I have made Saul king,'" God said, "'because he has turned away from me and has not carried out my instructions '"(15:11). When Samuel received this message, he was terribly grieved. We read that he "was troubled and he cried out to the LORD all that night" (15:11).

We're not told the specific emotions Samuel felt at this moment. Was he hurt? Sad? Depressed? Angry? No doubt, Samuel felt all of these negative emotions. After all, he had devoted a tremendous amount of energy and commitment walking Saul through the process of becoming king. He had clearly warned him to always obey God.

One thing is clear. Samuel was not using this opportunity to get even with Saul for replacing him as the leader in Israel. His motives were pure. More likely, Samuel was terribly distressed because he knew this was the "end of the line" for Saul. He understood enough of God's nature to know that the Lord's patience had run out and this was Saul's "Waterloo." It was over!

Samuel's mind had to have reflected back on his experience with his old friend and mentor, Eli. When just a young teen, God had spoken to Samuel and had told him to deliver a very painful message of judgment on this old man and his family. And now, once again Samuel was left with a very difficult and sad responsibility—to communicate with Saul that no matter how much he asked for forgiveness and pleaded for another opportunity, God had made up His mind and would not respond to his pleas.

What an incredible "Catch 22"! On the one hand, Samuel was caught between a man he had taught, prayed for, and hoped would succeed. On the other hand, as a prophet, he was faced with the awesome responsibility to pronounce judgment on Saul. At the human level, his back was against the wall—and Saul had put him there. He had taken advantage of Samuel's loyalty and God's grace. To be true to the God he loved and served, this old prophet had no choice but to obey the Lord. No wonder he must have felt intense frustration and anger. To literally cry out "all night" long indicates deep anxiety and hurt. Knowing Samuel, he may have even asked God for mercy on Saul—but clearly God would have said "no."

The Ultimate in Arrogance

Samuel wasted no time. He knew what he had to do. He rose early the next day "and went to meet Saul." But when he arrived he discovered the king had moved on to Carmel where he had "set up a monument in his own honor." He had then gone "on down to Gilgal" (15:12).

Imagine how Samuel must have felt when he arrived in Carmel and saw what Saul had done. How quickly this young Benjamite had succumbed to pride of the worst sort! It's not wrong to give honor to others when honor is due. And it's not wrong to accept honor when honor is due. But for Saul to build a monument to honor himself was the ultimate in arrogance. Could this be the same man who had "hidden himself among the baggage" (10:22b) because he was fearful to assume the role as king of Israel? Unfortunately, Saul had deteriorated spiritually—which was just the beginning of a terrible spiral downward that eventually led him to commit suicide!

When Samuel eventually caught up with Saul, the dialogue between them speaks volumes regarding what had happened to this man's spiritual perspectives. Let's listen in on a conversation filled with intense communication. Samuel was direct and uncompromising—and angry. Saul's responses were filled with nervousness, excuses, rationalizations, defensiveness, and deceit.

An Intense Conversation[1]
(1Samuel 15:13–30)

Saul: The Lord bless you! I have carried out the LORD's instructions.

Samuel: What then is this bleating of sheep in my ears? What is this lowing of cattle that I hear?

Saul: The soldiers brought them from the Amalekites; they spared the best of the sheep and cattle to sacrifice to the LORD your God, but we totally destroyed the rest.

Samuel: Stop! Let me tell you what the LORD said to me last night.

Saul: Tell me.

Samuel: Although you were once small in your own eyes, did you not become the head of the tribes of Israel? The LORD anointed you king over Israel. And he sent you on a mission, saying, "Go and completely destroy those wicked people, the Amalekites; make war on them until you have wiped them out." Why did you not obey the LORD? Why did you **pounce** on the plunders and do evil in the eyes of the LORD?

Saul: But I did obey the Lord. I went on the mission the LORD assigned me. I completely destroyed the Amalekites and brought back Agag their king. The soldiers took sheep and cattle from the plunder, the best of what was devoted to God, in order to sacrifice them to the LORD your God at Gilgal.

Samuel: Does the Lord delight in burnt offerings and sacrifices as much as in obeying the voice of the Lord?

To obey is better than sacrifice, and to heed is better than the fat of rams.

For rebellion is like the sin of divination, and arrogance like the evil of idolatry.

Because you have rejected the word of the LORD, he has rejected you as king.

Saul: I have sinned. I violated the LORD's command and your instructions. I was afraid of the people and so I gave in to them. Now I beg you, forgive my sin and come back with me, so that I may worship the LORD.

Samuel: I will not go back with you. You have rejected the word of the LORD, and the LORD has rejected you as king over Israel!"

At this point, Samuel turned to walk away from Saul. In desperation, Saul grabbed the hem of this old prophet's robe, and as Samuel turned to leave, the garment tore. Turning to Saul, Samuel turned this prophetic event into a pointed metaphor:

Samuel: The LORD has torn the kingdom of Israel from you today and has given it to one of your neighbors—to

> one better than you. He who is the Glory of Israel does not lie or change his mind; for he is not a man, that he should change his mind.

Saul: I have sinned. But please honor me before the elders of my people and before Israel; come back with me, so that I may worship the LORD your God.

A Broken Relationship

The end of this story blends compassion with judgment. Samuel honored Saul's last request. But perhaps his motives were mixed—to grant Saul one last moment of glory, but to also carry out a terrible responsibility—to execute Agag, the evil Amalekite king who had himself murdered many innocent women and children (15:33). Perhaps this is another reason Samuel was so displeased with Saul's behavior. He had to step in and carry out the terrible task that God had given to Saul as a military leader.

We're not told how long Samuel lived after these events. We simply read that he returned to Ramah and "Saul went up to his home in Gibeah" (15:34). What must have grieved Samuel more than anything is that he never saw Saul's face again (15:35) and once again we see Samuel's true pastoral heart. He "mourned" for Saul. He was deeply saddened over this turn of events. Though we can't understand totally how God must have felt, we simply read that "the LORD was grieved that he had made Saul king over Israel" (15:35).

A Final Major Task

Samuel's ministry was not ended in Israel. God chose him to anoint David as the new king. Though Samuel didn't live to see the day David would actually take over his position, he learned a great lesson about men God chooses to serve Him.

When evaluating each of the sons of Jesse as they passed before him, "the LORD said to Samuel," 'Do not consider his appearance or his height . . . . The LORD does not look at the things man looks at. Man looks at the outward appearance, but the LORD looks at the heart'" (1 Sam. 16:7).

Becoming God's Man Today

Principles to Live By

What can we learn from this final installment in the life of Samuel, particularly regarding his relationship with Saul? Following are some very important principles for anyone in the service of the King of Kings:

Principle 1. Living a godly life, particularly when we take a stand for righteousness and speak the truth in love, does not mean we will be liked and loved by everyone, including other Christians.

Confronting sin in the lives of fellow believers is probably the most difficult task we will ever face. For one thing, there is always the possibility we'll be rejected. As we've seen, this created a great deal of pain for Samuel. When Saul turned his back on this old prophet, who was his greatest supporter and prayer warrior, it added "insult to injury." He'd already felt rejection from the leaders in Israel when they replaced him. Now to be rejected by the king himself was a very difficult and painful experience.

A Matter of Life and Death

Think for a moment how Samuel must have felt when God asked him to go to Bethlehem to look for the man God had already chosen to replace Saul. "How can I go?" he responded, "Saul will hear about it and kill me!" (16:2). The task God asked Samuel to perform was a matter of life and death!

Fortunately, most of us will never face this kind of intense rejection when we confront sin in a Christian brother's life. But if we truly love someone, we'll take Paul's words seriously in his letter to the Galatians, regardless of another person's response: "Brothers, if someone is caught in a sin, you who are spiritual should restore him gently. But watch yourself, or you also may be tempted. Carry each other's burdens, and in this way you will fulfill the law of Christ" (Gal. 6:1–2).

Principle 2. One of the most subtle sins that leads to spiritual deterioration is pride.

This was the beginning of Saul's downfall. Though he began as a very humble man, he couldn't handle success. Sadly, he failed to realize that it was God who granted him victory over his enemies.

The Bible clearly warns against pride. This is why Paul cautioned Timothy against putting a new Christian in a place of primary leadership in the church. Regarding eldership, he wrote, "He must not be a recent convert, or he may become conceited and fall under the same judgment as the devil" (1 Tim. 3:6).

This is a principle, however, that applies to all Christians. Listen to Paul's words to the Philippians: "Do nothing out of selfish ambition or vain conceit, but in humility consider others better than yourselves. Each of you should look not only to your own interests, but also to the interests of others" (Phil. 2:3–4).

And who can forget the succinct Proverb that summarizes Saul's downfall: "Pride goes before destruction, a haughty spirit before a fall" (Prov. 16:18).

Principle 3. When we are veering from the path of biblical righteousness, God normally demonstrates His love and grace by sending initial warnings.

God did this for Saul. When he failed the first time, God warned him through Samuel. The message was sobering— that Saul's kingdom would not endure. But God did not say He would reject him without giving him a second chance.

This is the history of God's love and grace, even in the Old Testament. He didn't destroy Jericho for seven days, and only after He had warned these people and instructed Israel to march around the city the first six days and seven times on the last day. Just so, God did not destroy the Amalekites without warning them through the great miracles He worked for Israel.

Today, God is still patient, waiting for men to turn from their sins. Listen to the apostle Peter: "The Lord is not slow in keeping his promise, as some understand slowness. He is patient with you, not wanting anyone to perish, but everyone to come to repentance" (2 Pet. 3:9).

Principle 4. Even partial obedience and a lack of repentance eventually leads to serious consequences.

Saul had to learn this lesson the hard way. Though God was very patient, and even promised to bless him in spite of Israel's sin in demanding a king, eventually He allowed Saul to suffer the consequences of his disobedience. When he attempted to give the appearance he was obeying God fully when he was not, he only added to his condemnation.

Does God's patience ever come to an end? In Saul's case, yes. There seems to be sins that turn our hearts to stone, causing us to ignore God's love and grace. When this happens, people no longer listen to the voice of the Spirit. Their consciences become seared and unresponsive to truth (1 Tim. 4:2). God gives "them over" to practice "the sinful desires of their hearts" (Rom. 1:24). He gives them over to "shameful lusts" and "to a depraved mind" (1:26–28).

We must remember, however, that God did not reject Saul as a person. Rather, he rejected him as king. Had Saul turned to God for personal forgiveness, he would have received that forgiveness—just as David did when he pleaded for mercy in spite of his horrible sins of adultery and murder. Unfortunately, Saul wanted to be forgiven and then immediately honored before the elders and all the people of Israel (1 Sam. 15:30). That opportunity was over for Saul. He paid a terrible price for his rebellion, which God called worse than the "sin of divination," or witchcraft (15:23). Sadly, his "arrogance" was "like the evil of idolatry."

Fortunately, God forgives all of us no matter what our sins. He will never turn a deaf ear to true repentance (Heb. 3:7–15). However, there are some sins that disqualify us from ever holding the same leadership positions again—especially when we've reached the pinnacle of trust, such as being a God-appointed king! Though the royalty in England seem to be bending the rules for Prince Charles, we can be sure he'll never have the respect he would have had if he had maintained high moral standards.

Principle 5. Pride and arrogance are usually manifested in threats, self-deception, rationalization, and outright lying.

This is graphically illustrated in Saul's life. When Samuel arrived on the scene, Saul tried to cover his guilt by telling the old prophet that he had "carried out the LORD's instructions" (1 Sam. 15:13). He tried to beat Samuel to the draw. Obviously, his statements were only partially true. He had lied.

When Samuel charged him with not destroying *all* the animals of the Amalekites, he used the excuse that the *soldiers* had "spared the best of the sheep and cattle" to be offered to the Lord as sacrifices (15:15). At this point, he blamed his military personnel for his own sin and offered a "spiritual reason" for his disobedience.

Furthermore, at this moment he felt so guilty he couldn't even address his sovereign as "the LORD my (our) God." Rather, he identified Jehovah as "the LORD your [Samuel's]

God!" Saul had definitely lost his intimacy with his Creator and couldn't even address Him as his own personal Lord.

When Samuel challenged his rebellion, Saul rationalized and told Samuel, "But I did obey the LORD" (15:20). Somehow, he thought that if he took the lives of all the Amalekites, he could at least save the king.

When he eventually admitted that he had sinned, he continued to blame the people. "I was afraid," he said. "So I gave into them" (15:24). This response also reflects rationalization. He did not take full responsibility for his actions. He was the king and "the buck stopped there"! When his back was against the wall, he once again admitted his sin but wanted to maintain a place of honor in Israel (15:30).

In the way men and women today, when they're caught in a sin, may acknowledge that sin—not because they're truly sorry for hurting God and others—but because they've been caught. They've lost prestige and position.

I've seen this happen to some of my closest friends. In fact, I've had to confront this kind of sin. On one occasion, I faced this problem with an associate, a man I had trusted deeply. Unfortunately, he had committed adultery over a lengthy period of time but eventually was caught. I'll never forget his tears as he pleaded for forgiveness and restoration.

Right then and there I forgave him and had hoped for eventual restoration. But a close pastor friend of mine warned me— based on his own experience—that this show of "repentance" may not have been real but only a cry of remorse because this person had lost face and position. Frankly, I didn't believe my friend. Somehow I knew this repentance was for real. But sadly, my friend's warning turned out to be true. Eventually this man who had wept tears of sorrow began to lie about the seriousness of his affair, hoping for a speedy restoration.

He was caught in this additional sin, but still continued to indulge in various forms of deception and deceit. Unfortunately, this man has suffered the consequences of his sins.

Yes, God forgives—but He responds to true godly sorrow. Thank God for His patience and grace!

Personalizing These Principles

Following are some questions to help you make these principles a part of your own life. Once again, ask the Holy Spirit for insight into the depths of your own heart.

1. To what extent are you willing to pay the price to confront sin—even in your closest friend?

   If you believe God wants you to do so, be sure to follow these biblical guidelines:

   - Check your own life first (Matt. 7:3–5).
   - If it's a personal offense against you, take the first step.
   - By going to that person alone (Matt. 18:15–17).
   - If it's a sin against God and the body of Christ, take several mature Christians with you, but go in a spirit of humility and with the purpose of restoration (Gal. 6:1–3).

2. To what extent has pride entered your heart, causing you to exalt yourself and operate with selfish motives?

3. To what extent are you veering from God's righteousness and taking advantage of His grace, not realizing that He is being patient with you and giving you a second chance?

4. To what extent are you engaging in partial obedience, assuming God is honoring you in what you're doing and ignoring what you have failed to do?

5. To what extent are you covering your sin with self-deception, rationalization, or outright dishonesty?

Set a Goal

This is a very personal assignment. What has the Holy Spirit revealed to your heart? Select the one area that needs the most attention and write out a personal goal:

_____

_____

_____

_____

Memorize the Following Scripture

For the word of God is living and active. Sharper than any double-edged sword, it penetrates even to dividing soul and spirit, joints and marrow; it judges the thoughts and attitudes of the heart.
HEBREWS 4:12

Growing Together

1. Would you share an experience in which you attempted to confront sin and experienced rejection? How did you feel? Would you use a different approach if you had it to do over again?

2. How have you observed a spirit of pride and arrogance leading a person into deeper patterns of sin? Would you feel free to share how this has happened in your own life?

3. How has God demonstrated His grace in your life when you veered from His path of righteousness?

4. How has partial obedience led you (or someone else) into even greater disobedience?

5. In what ways have you observed sinful actions leading someone into self-deception, rationalization, and even lying? Would you feel free to share how this has hap-

pened to you?

6. What has ministered to you the most in this study of Samuel's life?

7. As we finish this study, in what way can we pray for you personally?

Endnotes

Chapter 1

1. Eugene H. Merrill, "1 Samuel," in *The Bible Knowledge Commentary, Old Testament,* ed. John F. Walvoord and Roy B. Zuck (Wheaton, Ill.: Victor Books, 1993), 431.

Chapter 2

1. *Dallas Morning News,* 9 November 1995, A-20.

Chapter 4

1. *Vision of Hope: An Anthology of Reflections,* William Sykes, compiler, (Oxford, England: The Bible Reading Fellowship, 1993), 285.

2. C. F. Keil and F. Delitzsch, *The Books of Samuel,* (Grand Rapids: Wm. B. Eerdman, 1985), 2:29.

Chapter 5

1. Keil and Delitzsch, *The First Book of Samuel,* 35.

2. *Unger's Bible Dictionary* (Chicago: Moody Press, 1961), 300.

Chapter 6

1. The "lamp of God" refers to the seven lamps that were lit every evening and burned through the night until the oil was used

up (Lev. 24:2–3). The reference to the fact that the lamp "had not yet gone out" could be translated "before the morning dawn" (Keil and Delitzsch, 48–49).

Chapter 7

1. Note the following comment by Keil and Delitzsch: "The two clauses, 'the word of Samuel came to all Israel' and 'Israel came out,' etc., are to be logically associated together in the following sense: 'at the word or instigation of Samuel, Israel went out against the Philistines to battle'" (Keil and Delitzsch, 52).

Dr. Eugene H. Merrill, Associate Professor of Semitics and Old Testament studies at Dallas Theological Seminary, agrees with Keil and Delitzsch. It's his opinion that the Hebrew grammar definitely supports the conclusion that it was Samuel's word, not God's word, that came to Israel. If this is true, it explains why the army of Israel was so soundly defeated by the Philistines.

2. We must not confuse God's omnipresence with His special manifestations. Though God is always present everywhere, He had chosen to reveal His glory in unique situations—such as in the burning bush when He spoke to Moses in the wilderness, at Mount Sinai when He revealed His law, and when He enthroned Himself between the cherubim in the Holy of Holies.

Chapter 8

1. For an exciting study regarding how to become the man God wants you to become, see *The Measure of a Man* by Gene Getz (Ventura, Calif.: Regal Books, 1995). After twenty years of very successful and continued use, this book has been completely rewritten and updated and serves as an excellent study on Christian maturity. Each chapter treats a measure of maturity as outlined by the apostle Paul in 1 Timothy 3 and Titus 1.

Chapter 9

1. Relative to the time Samuel became an official judge in Israel, Keil and Delitzsch add this helpful note: "With the calling of the people to Mizpah and the victory at Ebenezer that had been obtained through his prayer, Samuel had assumed the government

of the whole nation; so that his office as judge dates from this period, although he had labored as prophet among the people from the death of Eli, and had thereby prepared the way for the conversion of Israel to the Lord." Keil and Delitzsch, 76.

Chapter 10

1. Many commentators conclude that this town was Ramah where Samuel lived. However, it's relatively clear from the text that Samuel was visiting this unnamed town (9:12). Furthermore, when Saul and his servant left this town to return home, the places cited do not correlate with the territory surrounding Ramah (10:2–5).

Chapter 11

1. See Gene A. Getz, *Joseph: Overcoming Obstacles through Faithfulness* (Nashville: Broadman and Holman Publishers, 1996), part of the *Men of Character* series.

2. See Gene A. Getz, *David: Seeking God Faithfully* (Nashville: Broadman and Holman Publishers, 1995), part of the *Men of Character* series.

Chapter 12

1. See Gene A. Getz, *Moses: Freeing Yourself to Know God* (Nashville: Broadman and Holman Publisher, 1997), part of the *Men of Character* series.

Chapter 13

1. The following conversation is exactly as it appears in 1 Samuel 15 in the NIV translation. Only descriptive phrases are omitted, such as "Saul said," "But Samuel said," etc.